FAMOUS MAGIC SECRETS

FAMOUS MAGIC SECRETS

COMPILED AND EDITED BY

WILL DEXTER

MEMBER OF THE INNER MAGIC CIRCLE

ABBEY   LIBRARY

LONDON

CONTENTS

INTRODUCTION

A DOZEN or more people have written this book. I've only gathered their stuff together (and apart from a little bludgeoning with blunt instruments on my part, they've been more or less willing to write a piece here and there for me).

So here and now I would like to thank most sincerely those kind friends who have (*a*) provided material such as tricks, etc., for this book; (*b*) promised to write material but haven't written it; (*c*) wished me well with the book; and (*d*) promised to borrow a copy if they could find someone willing to lend it to them. Nice people, all of them (except So-and-so and You-know-who), but, dear reader, not nearly so nice as you, who have possibly bought a copy with real money.

And so this book is for *you*, you dear good soul, and you too, and you over there in the corner. It's for all of you.

That's why that fine fellow the publisher (who's actually paying me money for writing it!) has called it *Everybody's Book of Magic*.

Read it, revel in it, and insist that all your friends buy a copy for themselves. The publisher will spare no effort to have more copies printed if there aren't enough to go round, so don't stint yourselves.

That's the introduction, then. Now get on with reading the book. And thanks for reading so far.

WILL DEXTER.

London, November 1955.

OVERTURE AND BEGINNERS, PLEASE!

THAT'S the cry of the call-boy you'll hear backstage when it's only minutes to opening time. The members of the orchestra have doffed their coats and slipped into their dinner jackets. They've unpacked their instruments and taken a last drag at their cigarettes, and in a moment they'll file out into the orchestra pit and the lights will be dimmed.

You yourself, on the other side of the footlights, are comfortably settled in your seat, programme in hand, and are waiting for the show to start.

As you wait for *this* show to start, will you kindly accept these few words you're reading now as the overture?

This is a book about magic and magicians. In it I hope you'll learn the difference between "doing tricks" and performing magic. It's a book, though, to be read in conjunction with other books—lots of other books—if you want to perform magic.

If this is your first introduction to magic in print, I'd better explain a few things first.

Take tricks, now. Among magicians there's a lot of disagreement about the use of the word. Some say the "trick" is the means whereby the mystery is accomplished. Others say the trick is the trick, and that's that. The first group will tell you that what *you* know as a trick should be called an "effect," a "problem," an "experiment," or something of that sort.

In reply, the second group will ask: Whoever heard of the Indian Rope "Effect" or the Three Card "Problem" or the Sawing a Lady in Half "Experiment"?

So, as it's more than likely that you, kind reader, are a member of the non-magical public who know a trick as a trick, shall we call a trick a trick? Right. *That's* settled, then.

Now about "amateur and professional status." In this book I've referred to professional magicians as those who perform magic for a living, and have used the term "amateur" to define those who use magic as a hobby. These latter may—and often do—earn quite considerable sums of money as fees for presenting magic privately in their spare time. Among magicians, such performers are known as semi-pros, but as it's an unwieldy term I've more often referred to them as amateurs. So that's the dividing line you'll find in

9

these pages: a professional magician does magic for a living, and an amateur does it in his spare time. Let's forget about earning money (and let's hope the Inland Revenue will eventually do the same for those of us who are, in our own language, "semi-pros" and in your language "amateurs").

One last word—this time about the tricks that are included in these pages.

Once you become a magician, you'll be impressed with the urgent desire to maintain secrecy about methods of performing tricks. That's a fine thing. If there were no secrets, there'd be precious little magic. But, on the other hand, if there were no books of magic, there'd be even fewer magicians. So let's view it broadly. In this book you may read how to perform a number of tricks. Having learnt them, keep the method of doing them secret.

And if that sounds paradoxical—after all, secrets are *disclosed in this book*! —remember that this book is written as an introduction to magic, and one of its objects is to teach the beginner some simple tricks. As he proceeds, the beginner will become aware that this is *not* a book containing the ultimate secrets of magic.

But if you like, and before the curtain goes up, I'll tell you the ultimate secret. It's a simple one, and one word contains it all.

The word?

PRACTICE.

CHAPTER ONE

AND IT WASN'T UP HIS SLEEVE AT ALL!

ONCE upon a time, you watched a magician for the first time. You were wise, you were smart, you were not to be fooled. "It's up his sleeve!" you called out gleefully, if you were of the age that calls out gleefully in public. "Mirrors," you whispered, if you were of more mature age. "Mirrors—and secret threads."

And then the magician introduced you to a mystery that did not depend upon the use of his sleeve (and, between ourselves, very few mysteries *do* depend upon a magician's sleeve) and could not be accomplished either by mirrors or secret threads. Indeed, reason how you would, *this* mystery could not be accomplished by any means—except magic.

In short, you were floored.

You remember? Of course you do. In fact, the chances are that you're still baffled, though by now you may have seen this particular mystery a score of times. You have your private theories, of course, and are prepared to debate them earnestly, should you ever find a conjurer who will discuss this classic of magic. Magnetism, you suspect, might have more than a little to do with it. And then, of course, you will wisely recall that "the quickness of the hand deceives the eye." Or perhaps you belong to the school that believes in . . .

What trick was it? I'm sorry. I thought you'd remember. We're talking of the Chinese Linking Rings, of course.

Ah! *Now* you remember! I knew you would!

Admit it, now. When the magician showed you those solid steel rings, perhaps allowing you to handle them for yourself, and then proceeded to link them together in the most incredible patterns, you were mystified, weren't you?

And, unless you've actually been initiated into the secret of their manipulation, you're still baffled, aren't you? Right?

Well now, you can cease your wondering at this stage, for I propose to let you into a secret. The Linking Rings are not controlled by magnetism at all. The quickness of the hand does not deceive the eye.

This trick is performed by sleight of hand, pure sleight of hand. On a big scale, but none the less—sleight of hand.

Next time you see this trick performed, admire the magician's skill, please. And if no further secret of his manipulation falls into your receptive mind, accord him a double measure of appreciation.

For it is a fact that the secret of the Chinese Linking Rings has never yet been broken by the inquiring layman. There have been explanations in print, of course. Most of them attach great importance to the theory that one of the rings is split. All right. Make yourself eight or ten steel rings, ten inches or so in diameter. Saw through one of them. There you are! You have a split ring!

Now go ahead. Link them all together into a chain. See? It can't be done, can it?

If you have the patience to carry out this experiment, you will learn another thing. While you may, up to a point, deceive the eye with some of your manipulations, you will not deceive the ear. A split ring, you will find, jangles most discordantly. The echoing, ringing peal from the perfect rings is suddenly and sadly cracked by the flat "Twang-g-g!" of the split ring.

Ah well! There goes another illusion!

Something like four centuries ago, a Dutch painter named Hieronimus Bosch painted a picture which he called "The Conjurer." A magician in a long red robe stands behind a table performing another classical feat of magic—the Cups and Balls. Against the side of the table leans a single ten-inch metal ring. A copy of that picture hangs on my wall as I write this chapter. When inspiration flags, I turn my desk light on the picture and scan it closely. I am looking—as hundreds of other magicians have looked in the past—for *the other seven rings*. I feel that, were the picture a little more clear, and its lighting a little less mysterious, those other seven rings are to be found somewhere among the painted magician's paraphernalia. It seems hard to believe that Hieronimus Bosch's travelling conjurer would have omitted the Linking Rings from his repertoire.

He may not have presented it as conjurers present it today, and it's pretty certain that he didn't call it the Chinese Linking Rings. But I'm sure that he *did* present it.

For, in one form or another, the Linking Rings may be said to date back for centuries. Nobody yet has tracked them down to their origin with any certainty, and I don't suppose anybody ever will. We know that they first came to Britain over a hundred years ago, when a troupe of Chinese jugglers and acrobats brought them to this country. Hence, no doubt, their "Chinese" tag.

To magicians, the beginnings of the trick are as mysterious as the performance of it is to the layman. I have heard it said that you may see the trick pictured on ancient Egyptian papyri. But I doubt it. The Linking Rings may date back so far, but it's more likely that they come from India than from Egypt—or China.

Their inception, I like to think, marks the time when magic broke away from the pagan temples and came out into the open light of day; when its practitioners depended more upon personal ability than upon dim-lit interiors and dim-witted audiences.

After all, if you are a follower of Baal, of Osiris, of Ahriman, or any of the scores of popular deities of man's dark past, you *expect* mysteries in your temple. You expect flames to leap from the empty bowl the priest holds; you expect massive stone portals to swing open at a trumpet call; you expect the sacred fountain to stop and start at command, and to pour out wine instead of water when the presiding Master bids.

Further, you expect these things to happen in a dim, religious light, and you would gladly stone a man who so much as suggested that the same dim light concealed the means whereby the mystery was accomplished.

And, of course, the sciences of hydraulic power, optics, pyrotechnics and acoustics not yet having been discovered to you, you cannot, whether you dare or not, attribute the flaming bowl, the gushing fountain, the opening door to any of these branches of learning.

But the priest who holds the fire bowl knows better, as he deftly tips a few drops of oil and water upon a pellet of sodium metal or potassium. And the unseen *deus ex machina* who pulls the lever which decants several hundred gallons of water down the chute which operates the stone doors knows better. So does the hidden accomplice who operates the plunger and turns the taps that help the fountain to function.

If you, as the patient and admiring worshipper at the shrines of Baal, of Osiris, of Ahriman, or a thousand other dark gods, express a wish to examine the fire bowl, or to go underground and look into the matter of the trick door or the obliging fountain, do you know what will happen? You'll figure prominently in the next sacrificial function. And, as far as you're concerned, that will be that.

There, as I pointed out above, will have gone another illusion, and there, too, will have gone another awkward, prying member of an unquestioning audience.

Incidentally (let us whisper it) there are more than a few "kiddies' entertainers" who, in their confidential moments, sigh for the days when a shrill scream of "It's up his sleeve!" would have meant another victim for the boiling oil.

But as things are—"Mustn't even make a face at 'em now," they will moan, agreeing, among themselves, that entertaining the dear kiddies sometimes means earning one's living the hard way.

It's a far cry from the dim, murky temples of the distant past to the glaring lights of the television studio. But magic has come all that way, and has never lost its way in the coming. Sometimes it's met with opposition, fostered by superstition as abysmal as that which once stood open-mouthed in the pagan temples. A few heads have fallen beside the way. A few miracle-workers have languished in the cooler, a few light-fingered performers have forfeited those fingers—and thumbs—to the public executioner. Sometimes it's been borrowed by unscrupulous devotees of various "religions"; sometimes it's been used—and successfully, too!—to prove this or that phenomenon of telepathy, telekinesis, or clairvoyance.

But it's still with us, this unique entertainment called magic. And today it's respectable, it's enjoyable—it's *fun*.

It's fun to watch, and it's fun to perform. It's fun to talk about, and it's fun to read about.

Once you become involved as far as the stage where you know other magicians, then you become one of their crazy brotherhood. And I use the word "crazy" in no derogatory sense (although most conjurers' wives solemnly believe that all magicians *are* crazy!) but to denote the world in which they live.

It's a world where a man spends months of his valuable time—usually leisure time, so doubly valuable—in planning a new way to make a card rise out of a pack of playing cards. A hidden thread will do the job simply and effectively, but he's a perfectionist, is your magician, and must devise a new, foolproof, imperceptible method of baffling not only the public but his brother magicians as well.

He'll talk about his researches to the next magician he meets, but the chances are that the other fellow has no patience with people who fuddle along trying to improve the Rising Cards. Now *he* (he'll tell you) is working on a new Floating Ball Illusion, and has been building and rebuilding it for a year or more. . . .

See what I mean by "crazy"?

And the magicians who read this while they wait for the glue to dry on their latest miracle ("Been working on it for six years, old boy") will no doubt hotly deny that these words apply to them. Others, yes. Us, no.

Ah well! Crazy or not, we love our hobby.

And this book is going to tell you something about us. If, at the end of it, you find yourself diligently practising one or other of the tricks I have persuaded good magical friends to write up for me . . . if you're in so far, then—Welcome, brother magician!

CHAPTER TWO

THIS IS AN AMATEUR'S WORLD!

TODAY the world of magic is an amateur's world. It wasn't always so. Time was when the magician was a dreaded figure, guarding secrets that would be regarded as elementary today, but which were the foundations of a terrible culture in ages past.

From the arch-priest sprang the seer. From the seer came the wise man. From the wonder-worker of the temples came, by long and devious routes, the *jongleur*, whose simple mysteries entertained the market-place crowds of the Middle Ages. And the *jongleur's* offspring were two—the juggler and the conjurer. Even now many people confuse the two. I called at a curio shop recently, seeking Chinese coins for a trick. The dealer, taking one look at me, said: "I can see you're not a collector. You want these for a juggling trick. We get a lot of jugglers in here after such things."

But the juggler and the conjurer went their separate ways centuries ago, and are now completely different entities.

While the juggler was training his children almost from birth in the extremely difficult art of unstable equilibrium, the conjurer passed his talents on to few. In the East, they were handed down from father to son for many generations, until today you will find a caste of conjurers in India. Their forefathers, back into the unfathomable past, have been conjurers, and their descendants will doubtless be conjurers, too.

What's more, they'll probably be doing the same tricks in a thousand years' time as their remote ancestors were performing in the past.

In Europe it's been different.

·Magic has lost its mysticism here, and is regarded purely as an entertainment. A magician may persuade his son that conjuring is a fascinating hobby, but it's more than likely that the son will see so much of conjuring at home that he'll go in for pigeon breeding or the musical glasses.

And so the magician, if he is to foregather with his kind, will join a magicians' club. If there isn't a club, then he'll form one, and that will be that.

A hundred years ago, the drawing-room conjurer was beginning to come into his own. Fifty years ago, the music-hall brought the Golden Age of magic, with such immortal performers as Chung Ling Soo, Houdini, Lafayette, Horace Goldin and a score of other top-liners. Now television has taken over from the music-hall.

What now?

Magicians believe that magic will really reappear as a leading art of entertainment when colour television becomes an established fact.

But until then, there'll be magicians in every town and village, conjurers who love their art and will carry the torch until magic comes back.

It mustn't be thought from that statement that magic is dead. It is as much alive today as ever it has been during the past century and more. But the number of professional conjurers has diminished sadly with the decline of the music-hall.

There have been amateur magicians for more than a century. Before then, there weren't many. With the coming of Robert-Houdin, the famous French magician in the nineteenth century, conjuring became really popular, and the amateur was born.

Today, as in the past, magic attracts a wide circle of amateurs. From all walks of life they come. Not many days ago, I saw a duke learning a card trick from a chimney-sweep—and, let me tell you, the chimney-sweep was by far the better magician!

Charles Dickens may have been the first of the magical dilettantes. In between writing his immensely long novels, acting in amateur theatricals, and travelling Europe with Forster, Charles Dickens found time to learn and perform many mysteries. Dickens was a man who by nature had to have an audience. His writings were—and are today—regarded as essential reading. His amateur theatrical work attracted such favourable notice that he could, had he wished, have made a fortune as an actor. His conjuring— as one would expect from such a thorough mind—was of equally high standard.

The art of magic appeals to a particular kind of man—the mind that must reason things out to its own satisfaction, and must prove and demonstrate the sequence of its findings to others.

That's rather a complicated way of putting it, perhaps, so let's say that the amateur conjurer *is* an amateur conjurer because he likes being one!

And if he's a good one other people, too, will like him to be a magician.

There's a freemasonry of magic which is universal. Go where you will, you will find that one magician always welcomes another, and extends the fullest hospitality to him. In many parts of the world I have proved this for myself. I've met fellow journalists in foreign cities who showed not the slightest interest in the fact that I followed the same calling as they. Frankly,

I showed equally little interest in them, too. But wherever I have mentioned conjuring to a magician, of any race, we've been brothers at once!

In other branches of entertainment there's often a barrier between the professional and the amateur, but not so in magic. The world of the professional singer is a different one from that of the amateur vocalist, and the two rarely meet. The circus acrobat has little in common with the physical culture student. And the professional actor has very little time indeed for the amateur.

But visit a professional magician in his dressing room at the theatre, and what will you find? One or more of the local amateur magicians are already there. They've seen the show from the front of the house, slipped round to the stage door as soon as the magician's turn was over—bother the rest of the show; they don't want to see *that!*—and there they stay for the evening.

What's more, they're made welcome there, for the professional magician was once an amateur himself, and he knows and appreciates the help he can get from the amateurs. Many a brilliant illusion has been planned on a dressing-room table, with a local amateur providing the basic idea.

The world of amateur magic contains some of the keenest brains in the world of everyday life. Doctors, lawyers, police officers, industrialists, bankers, scientists and others of the same mental calibre devote their leisure hours to the hobby of conjuring, and bring to the art the benefit of their highly trained minds.

You'll find amateur magicians in the House of Lords—Lord Amwell has written text-books on magic—and you'll find them behind shop counters such as that of Eric Newton, of Nottingham, who keeps a modest grocer's shop. You'll find them throughout the Services and in the Civil Service— Lieut.-Colonel Lewis Ganson, an internationally known expert on sleight of hand, and Victor Peacock, prominent investigator of fraudulent occultism, are two examples from those sources. You'll find them in the Church—as witness the Rev. George Arrowsmith, Rector of Torquay, and the Abbé Brehamel, of Paris. In Royal Houses you'll find them, too. The late Maharajah of Jodhpur was an ardent amateur magician, and has demonstrated his skill at public shows in London for the Magic Circle. Prince Knud of Denmark is a keen member of Denmark's only magical club.

It's a wide territory, this world of magic, with no national boundaries, no class distinctions, and no racial discrimination. Its friendly democracy could teach much to the governments of that wider world in which we all live.

CHAPTER THREE

SO YOU WANT TO BE A MAGICIAN?

ALL right. So you want to be a magician? First of all, though, let's get this clear: what *sort* of magician do you want to be? A man who does tricks? But he's not a magician—he's only a man who does tricks.

You see, there's a world of difference between just *doing* tricks and making them entertaining. And today, a magician must be entertaining. It wasn't necessarily always so. Not many years ago, before popular entertainment came within the reach of everybody, a magician could get by with his tricks and illusions alone. There were no films, no radio, no television, not so many theatres as were to come later. The magician was mainly to be seen at private parties (where, incidentally, he reaps a pretty rich harvest today), and people just didn't have a chance of establishing a standard by which to judge their entertainment. But today, with television in most homes, cinemas in every main road, a number of variety theatres (though sadly depleted) still flourishing, the public expect more than mere mysteries.

They expect—and demand—to be entertained.

That doesn't mean that the magician must be a comedian. Many of the finest conjurers today never crack a joke in their performances. But they do infuse entertainment into them. You come away from seeing them thinking: "That fellow would have entertained me even if he'd done no magic." You feel that the performer you've just seen could be equally good as an after-dinner speaker, as a lecturer, as a raconteur, as almost anything that would hold your attention and send you away pleased.

The man with the bag of tricks, who presents them baldly as tricks and nothing more, is merely showing puzzles. "I can do it and you can't" is his theme.

And so the skilled magician today owes much of his success to the fact that he can entertain as well as mystify.

There's a large body of magical opinion even today that denies this necessity to entertain. Those who uphold it will point to some heroic figure of the Golden Age of magic, and will try to prove that *his* first aim was to mystify, rather than to entertain.

"Look at Houdini!" one of them said to me the other day. "Did Houdini place entertainment before mystery?"

It wasn't a very happy choice, selecting Houdini to support this fallacious argument. Houdini *did* entertain his audience—with suspense. The mystery was only a secondary element in his shows. The crowds who flocked to see him escape from a milk churn filled with water didn't much care *how* he did it. They went along to see whether he *would* do it. When Houdini hung, head downwards and tightly strapped in a strait-jacket, from the parapet of a sky-scraper, do you think the crowds in the street cared how he got out of the strait-jacket? What they were asking themselves was: "*Will* he get out of it?"

If Houdini had stuck to card tricks, which was one of his first loves, do you suppose you'd have heard of his name today?

Early in his career, Houdini* found that suspense paid handsomely. His public performances depended almost entirely on the atmosphere of suspense he created in the minds of the spectators.

In one of his illusions, Houdini would escape from goodness knows how many bonds, shackles, chains and handcuffs while imprisoned in a sealed mailbag placed in a locked chest behind screens on the stage. The escape took a matter of seconds only. But Houdini didn't rush out from behind the screens then, panting with the triumph of having done the job of escaping in record time. Decidedly not.

Instead, he would escape, take an evening newspaper from his pocket, and read it patiently behind the cover of the screens on the stage, and would only come out when the audience had been worked into a veritable frenzy of suspense.

If he'd popped out a few seconds after being imprisoned, the illusion would have gone. It would all have seemed too easy to do. But by waiting behind the screens for ten or twenty minutes, he built up terrific suspense, and had the spectators really concerned for his safety. And the applause that roared out when he *did* reappear wasn't entirely a tribute to Houdini's skill in getting out of his bonds; much of it was given in a spirit of pure relief that he *had* got out.

Now let's go to the other end of the magical scale—to the young schoolboy who has come into possession of a trick. He shows it to you once. You admire it, secretly trying to puzzle out how it's done.

He sees that you're baffled, so he does the trick again, on the principle of what's done twice must be twice as baffling. This time you catch a glimpse

* Real name, Erich Weiss. The son of a rabbi, young Weiss took his name from Robert-Houdin, famous French magician of a century ago.

of some secret movement, and you begin to see how the trick could be done. But you're polite, so you applaud again.

What then?

Oh dear!

The wretched boy does the trick yet again.

By this time, you're not baffled; you're bored. You know how the trick's done (secretly, perhaps, you'd like to handle the trick and try it yourself) but you *really* don't want to see it again, thank you very much.

Much less would you pay money to see it done again. But now ask yourself what you *do* pay money to see, in the way of magic. Why, you've seen Kalanag every time he's been to the local Empire. You may even remember having seen David Devant a dozen or so times. And yet, each time you saw these fine performers, you saw tricks and illusions that you'd seen before.

They'd entertained you, though. They'd certainly shown you puzzles, just as your schoolboy friend showed you a puzzle, but the subtle difference is that you'd like to see *their* puzzles again. The reason is that Kalanag and Devant had dressed up their puzzles in the rich garments of entertainment, and you've been content to pay good money to see them again and again.

I stress this need for entertainment, as well as mystery, because it leads naturally to the first kind of magic I'd like to describe for you—pocket tricks.

Probably the first trick anyone acquires is a pocket trick of some sort. And pocket tricks are—let's face it—little different, in themselves, from puzzles.

There isn't a great deal of difference between the trick in which the conjurer mysteriously makes two closed safety pins link together and one of those old-fashioned wire puzzles which only the possessor of the instructions could disentangle.

The chief difference is, of course, that the safety pins are ordinary, everyday articles, such as you would not expect to be associated with mystery, whereas the wire puzzle is a wire puzzle only, and could never be described as anything else.

But see a first-class conjurer present the mystery of the Linking Pins, and you will see a miniature illusion that is entertaining as well as mystifying. See a novice present the same trick, and you see a variation of a wire puzzle.

We *must* draw a distinction between the magician and the man-who-does-tricks.

The pocket-trick field is an incredibly wide one. Bobby Bernard, a young member of the Magic Circle, collects pocket tricks. At present, his collection numbers something over seven hundred—all different. In ten years' time it will probably number twice as many.

So, you see, you have plenty of choice if you decide to go in for pocket tricks.

You may pay as little as sixpence for a pocket trick bought on a market stall, or you may pay as much as £5 for a skilfully designed and finely made piece of mechanism that would, say, make a finger ring jump from one hand to the other. The expert will think nothing of paying an average of £1 each for his pocket tricks. But that need not dismay the modest beginner. For the same £1 that buys one trick for the expert, the novice can buy a dozen different, if less ambitious, pocket tricks.

There's a well-known pocket trick known as the Chinese Compass, among other names. In effect, it's a small dial made of plastic, wood or cardboard, on which an arrow seems to point in any direction at the will of the conjurer. You could buy one of these for half a crown. You could also make an excellent Chinese Compass for the price of four square inches of thin cardboard and a pencil with which to draw the arrow.

The best presentation of the Chinese Compass was one shown to me by a well-known Nottingham magician, who used one of those cardboard mats you find on bar counters, and a stick of grease-paint to draw the arrow. In my pocket at the time I had a handsome plastic Chinese Compass, which had cost me ten shillings. Yet my friend's impromptu version of the trick, combined with his clever and entertaining patter, made me feel like throwing away my splendid ten-bob model.

Money, then, need mean little when the performer has the ability to entertain.

Pocket tricks demand one important consideration: you must have variety in them.

Many tricks depend upon the spectator's following one of three items. An example of this is the notorious Three Card Trick, or "Find the Lady." Another example is known as the Rattle Bars. Of three little bars, one rattles when it is shaken, and the spectator is invited to spot which bar is the rattler. There is also a trick with three bells, one of which rings, while the others are silent. The old racecourse trick with the three walnut shells and the pea is another example of the same effect. Nowadays, a sophisticated version of the same thing is known as the Wandering Lipsticks; again, one rattles and the others don't.

As far as the spectator is concerned, *these are all the same trick*. Each is worked by a different method, but method doesn't interest the spectator. What captures his attention is *effect*.

Too many amateur conjurers completely overlook this fact. It's quite usual to see an inexperienced performer show, say, the Three Card Trick, the Rattle Bars, and the Walnut Shell Trick, one after the other. Because the methods of working are different, he regards each as a different trick—but not so the spectator.

There are so many, many pocket tricks on the market and described in books that there is no excuse for failing to vary one's repertoire, not only as to method but as to effect.

In the matter of pocket tricks, there's another important aspect to consider: does the trick need a performing surface, such as a table or counter, or can it be done entirely in the hands?

Edward Victor, one of the Magic Circle's vice-presidents and one of the world's leading sleight of hand experts, specialises in tricks that can be worked entirely in the hands, without any table or other surface. It's a good policy, too, for such tricks can be performed anywhere. Nothing is more irritating to the patient spectator than to see a trick proceed half-way and then to be told: "Oh! Sorry! I'll have to start again—look, let's drag this table over here."

A good showman would never make the mistake of starting a trick without seeing the whole performance through in his mind's eye. He would never start a trick without having everything ready and all the conditions perfect—or as perfect as he can make them. If a table is needed, he'll see that the trick's started where there *is* a table. If more than one spectator has to take part, he won't start the trick until he has enough spectators.

I've found that it's a good practice to have one's table tricks kept separately in the pocket from one's hand tricks. I carry my pocket tricks in two leather tobacco pouches, one in each side pocket of the jacket. The left pocket carries tricks that can be done anywhere, for the apparatus is held in the hands all the time. In the right pocket is the pouch with the table tricks in it.

As time goes on, the amateur magician finds that he's accumulated many pocket tricks. Too often, he carries them all around with him. That's neither good for his suit nor for his reputation. It's far better to carry, say, four hand tricks and four table tricks. These, with a pack of cards, will allow a nice little programme to be planned, and will keep a few tricks in reserve.

A first-class programme of pocket tricks could be assembled for £2 or less, but the advice of an experienced magician should be taken when buying. The dealer will rarely disclose the secret of a trick before selling it, and many small tricks are worked with the same apparatus. As a result, the unsuspecting novice may find that the half-dozen packets he's bought, each for a separate trick, contain identical apparatus. The experienced conjurer knows pretty thoroughly how each trick is done and what apparatus is needed for it, and so can save the novice's pocket where duplicated apparatus will perform several tricks.

The mention of table tricks leads straight into the next type of magic—Close-up Magic.

This is a branch of the conjurer's art which is exceedingly popular today, and it calls for a moderately high degree of skill. It may not be the execution of the tricks themselves that demands skill; it's more likely to be the conditions under which the magician is working. For close-up magic—almost always performed seated at a table—really *is* close up. And for that reason each move must be perfect, each sleight faultless, and each piece of apparatus always under perfect control.

Another vital essential—the magician's hands must be in tiptop condition. If he has the unfortunate habit of biting his nails, for instance, then he would be better advised to practise his magic from a platform, where the spectators are farther away from him and cannot see his hands so closely. When the eyes of his audience are perhaps less than three feet away from his hands, those hands must be in good shape.

Close-up magic is seen at its best in the field of sleight of hand. There is always the serious risk that if faked apparatus is used, or a mechanical device is needed, one of the people sitting at the table will pick it up and examine it.

One of the most skilful close-up conjurers I've seen is Gus Southall, whose home is at Flixton, Manchester. When the Magic Circle Golden Jubilee celebrations were televised, Gus Southall was selected out of the many hundreds of magicians present to perform his close-up magic before the television cameras for the B.B.C. And there is no stiffer test of talent than to perform magic right under the all-seeing lens of the television camera.

Fortunately, Gus Southall is not only a sleight of hand expert but also a shrewd student of human psychology. For this occasion he relied entirely on his sleight of hand and psychological cunning, backing his own manipulative skill against the keen eye of the cameras. He knew exactly what he could do with his hands and his quick brain, and he may well have felt that he did not care to rely upon a piece of tricked mechanism that might choose that one occasion to break down.

The close-up magician relies very greatly on his knowledge of psychology. This he applies in several directions, primarily as misdirection. By a glance of his eye he can make the eyes of his audience look in any direction he chooses. While he looks at his hands, the audience will look at his hands. But the moment he looks a spectator in the eye and addresses him, that spectator will lift his own eyes and look the magician in the face. The rest of the audience will look from magician to spectator, according to who is talking. And meanwhile the conjurer performs his sleight or carries out some other secret operation with his hands. He is safe in doing so, for he has misdirected the eyes and attention of the audience from his hands.

This may seem hard to believe, but it's easy to prove. Show a person a trick, and tell him that he *must* watch your hands closely. When you want him to take his eye off your hands look him straight in the eye and declare: "You're *not* watching my hands, as I told you!" He will at once look up at your face, and will no doubt insist that his eyes have never left your hands for a moment.

Misdirection is a powerful weapon, but it must be used wisely. If the secret move the magician must make occupies more than a brief second, or if it calls for wide gestures, he must adopt more positive misdirection than merely changing the direction of the spectator's gaze. He might, for example, drop something on the floor, and, in stooping to pick it up, perform his secret sleight. Or he could hand a piece of apparatus to a spectator—a piece of apparatus that might be suspected by the audience. As soon as the spectator takes this in his hands, the other spectators will concentrate their whole attention on it.

"Will he discover its secret?" they will ask themselves, watching with interest as their companion investigates the apparatus.

There is an interesting little trick called the Blondin Cube in which a small brass cube, threaded on a string, can be made to slide down the string, or to stop at any stage in its fall, at the conjurer's command. This trick is an invaluable aid to misdirection, I find. I perform the trick, and show that the cube will either run down the string or stop, just as I wish. I then hand it to some member of the audience seated round the table. He *cannot* make the cube stop in the course of its fall, and his efforts to do so always—*always*—attract the complete and undivided attention of the audience.

At different stages in the programme I hand the cube to other spectators. Each time, without exception, the misdirection thus obtained enables me to do almost anything I need to do, completely unobserved.

Misdirection should be *cultivated*. In other words, the means of employing it must be used naturally for their natural purposes. In one trick that I perform, I have to change one small item for a prepared duplicate. I found that the best way to operate the change was by hiding the duplicate object on the edge of my chair seat. From time to time, I draw my chair a little nearer to the table, or a little farther away. The spectators are thus accustomed to my hands dropping to the edges of the chair seat to move it. And so, when I have to make the switch (magicians always refer to an exchange of articles as a switch) I can do so without suspicion. The movement needed is a wide, sweeping one, but because the audience are accustomed to it it passes unnoticed.

Psychology is used to sharpen another weapon in the close-up man's armoury—suggestion.

For instance, we discussed an example of misdirection in which the spectator was allowed to handle a piece of "suspect" apparatus. The magician has planted in the spectator's brain the idea that the piece is suspect—that it might be faked, and that the spectator must on no account handle it. He could do this by seeming reluctant to let it be handled, or by pretending to conceal it, or, more simply still, by laying it on the edge of the table near himself, while other equipment is spread out near to the spectators. The acute spectator will quite probably demand: "I wish you'd let us see that little box (or whatever) that you're trying to keep so secret there!"

Presto! The suggestion has worked!

Another direction in which psychological suggestion is used is in downright lying!

But after all, it's a harmless lie, as a rule, and one that brightens up the trick.

You may have seen that astonishing trick in which a borrowed, signed £1 note is made to vanish, and is found in a metal tube that has already been examined and found quite empty. This is the Bill Tube, so called because it originated in America, where they refer to paper money as bills.

The tube looks like nothing the ordinary person has ever seen before. If the magician is not careful, the spectators will at once realise that here is something *that was made specially for the trick.*

And that's fatal to the illusion we want to create.

So it becomes necessary to explain away this metal tube. It has to be identified as a tube that is really used for something else, something quite legitimate if not fully understood.

The tube is small, but massively constructed. It has a screw top, through which runs a screw. On the end of the screw, as often as not, you will find a small padlock.

What, I asked myself when I bought it, could this tube *ever* be used for? It had to be given a spurious identity that would tally with its appearance. It's a solid, well-secured tube, so you'd expect it to be used for containing something of great value. Money? No. There are boxes and wallets for money. Gold? No. Radium? That was it!

So I tell my audience that the tube is the outside casing of a container for carrying radium needles. The inside shell, of course, I tell them, is made of lead, but as it's always radio-active after use it's been destroyed and I can't show them that piece of the container. However, it doesn't matter; all I needed was a strong tube into which nothing could pass, and from which nothing could escape, once the top had been screwed on and locked.

Then we get on with the trick.

The fact is, though, that the tube is made for this particular trick and for nothing else in the world. The "explanation" as to its real use serves two purposes. It identifies the tube as something more or less normal, and it provides the spectators with something to think and talk about.

When they are told, casually but seriously, that this thing is used for carrying radium needles, they show the greatest interest, and often talk about it afterwards.

It's a lie, but it's been a most useful lie!

Tsk! Tsk! As David Nixon confesses so contritely in his "explained" paper-tearing trick: "It's a dirty business, this magic!"

Having watched hundreds of close-up magicians at work, I have a word of warning to those deciding to take up this branch of conjuring: Don't overdo it. After four or five tricks, FINISH. Leave them wanting more. Much the same applies to all magic, but in the case of pocket tricks and close-up magic the warning is especially necessary. It's so easy to carry about all the tricks you own—they're so portable—that you may be tempted to go on performing all night. From then on, you'll be a marked man, and your friends will avoid you!

What would it cost you to put together a couple of good close-up programmes? That's almost impossible to answer. If you want to go in for the apparatus kind of trick, it's like the pocket-trick field; you can pay anything from a shilling to £10 for a good close-up trick. But the advice given by most close-up conjurers is this: buy good up-to-date books and study them. Learn to be a competent sleight of hand performer, and do your close-up magic with everyday objects—cards, coins, bank-notes, handkerchiefs, finger rings, and the like. Don't buy "messy" tricks, such as those using many pieces of apparatus for the same trick. Try to avoid tricks using liquids that might slop about. Keep the whole routine simple, using simple things, and get a direct effect rather than a prolonged series of climaxes.

From close-up table magic, let's go on to what's known as "Club Magic." This is a type of magic suitable for smallish audiences in a confined space, such as, for instance, the floor-show entertainment one sees in a cabaret performance.

It ranks midway between the close-up variety and the platform performance. Here, more apparatus can safely be used, and the effects should be larger than those used by the close-up man.

By larger, I don't mean that larger pieces of apparatus need necessarily be used. The Ring on Wand, for instance, needs nothing more than a handkerchief, a wand, pencil or chopstick, and a borrowed finger ring. But its effect is much wider than a trick with the same items performed at a table. The magician moves about more, the spectators, to some extent, also move about, and the climax is more dramatic than could be obtained at a table.

Many professional magicians who work floor shows try to make the most of this widening of effect, while using only the bare minimum of props. The result is that they can sometimes carry their whole act in their pockets.

My friend Bertram Millidge, of Nottingham, has a delightful cabaret act, in which he makes his entrance carrying a ten-inch steel ring and a large silk handkerchief. The rest of the act is contained on a small tray on his equally small table. In the course of this act, he performs an apparent miracle with nothing but the ring and the handkerchief. He then produces, seemingly from the folds of the handkerchief, a large birdcage, as big as a football (and if you don't think that's very big for a birdcage, believe me, it's a *terrific* size for a conjurer's birdcage!). There follow a couple of clever tricks with a pack of cards, and the act concludes with the famous Linking Rings, at which Millidge is a past master of great skill.

This is what's known as a "clean" act.

At the other end of the scale there is the conjurer who struggles on with a large draped table and a couple of trays of bulky miscellaneous apparatus, which he usually has to stow away on borrowed chairs or on the floor. In the course of his show—which is generally a long one, alas!—he produces things and has to find somewhere to lay them down. He makes things vanish, and then has to find a place to park the apparatus into which they've vanished— a place where no nosey member of the audience can inspect the apparatus. He has silk handkerchiefs of varying shades of grubbiness draped over everything. He may have someone fling a pack of cards at him so that he can catch one on the point of a sword. The whole act is like an overloaded Christmas tree, and he leaves the floor burdened with bits and pieces that scatter in a trail behind him as he walks off. He will, no doubt, leave his pack of cards strewn over the room where it landed when he did his Card Sword trick. After all, playing cards are cheap enough—why should he bother to pick 'em up?

That's a messy act. Messy acts are the bane of the good conjurer's life. Let an entertainment organiser book one messy act, and there'll be no more conjurers for *that* organiser. In other words, not only does the messy magician kill his own market, but he makes it unattainable for more efficient magicians.

There's no need for the club magician to present a messy act. There are literally thousands of good, entertaining tricks for this sort of performance. It's the easiest thing in the world to build up a club act that is self-contained and portable.

Which brings us to the question of "setting." Many tricks, such as the Chinese Linking Rings and the Cups and Balls, are entirely self-contained and require no setting before they are presented. Others have to be prepared in some way before they can be shown. One such trick, which requires to be set before each performance, is the Vanishing Birdcage. The full preparation for this startling trick must be made in private.

The ideal performance, from the club magician's point of view, would be that using only self-contained, non-setting tricks. There's a snag there, however. Some of the most spectacular tricks are those which must be set before each performance. So we must regard the necessity for setting as one of the chores that must be done if we want to show these tricks. Not all of us have the skill to perform only with self-contained apparatus. Not all audiences, either, can appreciate such skill when they see it.

So a few spectacular tricks that need to be set beforehand can make a wise admixture to the programme completed by sheer digital skill and sleight of hand.

The club show, or floor show, is one of the most pleasant to work, but it has a serious drawback.

The angles have to be studied extremely carefully. In other words, while a trick might succeed on a stage, where the whole audience is in front of the performer, it may well be impossible to show it at all with the audience all round the magician. There may be some secret lurking at the back of the apparatus—a large hole scooped out of the back of a box, a duplicate piece of equipment hidden behind something else, or a shelf that should be concealed at the back of a table. There may be some sleight that it is impossible to perform with spectators behind the performer. The Back and Front Palm with cards, for example, must never, never be seen from the back! It may be, too, that the trick demands absolute stillness of the magician while he faces in one direction. If so, those behind him just don't see what's going on.

Not always does the club magician have to perform in the middle of the floor, though. It is often possible for him to establish his position with his back to a wall (no mirrors on the wall, please!) at one end of the room.

However, this question of angles need never stand in the way of the conjurer performing with the audience all round him. Again, there are more than enough first-rate tricks that can be worked under these conditions. But for a magician to walk on to the middle of a ballroom floor and then to demand a complete reshuffle of the audience so that nobody is behind him is the worst possible commendation of his skill. He should make sure that he has suitable tricks before he starts his performance. The fact that he insists on displacing the spectators sitting behind him proves to them that he has something to hide. And they'll watch all the more closely when they know that! The magician will probably learn after his show that one or more spectators have crept round to get a privileged view from the back, and that they've been delightedly signalling all his secret moves to their friends in front.

Many tricks that can be performed with the audience all round one can also be performed equally successfully on the platform. But some floor-show tricks just don't go down well from the stage. There's the matter of getting spectators up to assist, for one thing. In the floor-show, the spectators are there all round the performer; they're easy of access and are ready and willing to help when they're invited.

But let the magician get up on a platform, with bright lights shining on him while the audience sit in concealing darkness, and it's a very different proposition. The problem of getting volunteer assistants can be a real problem then. For that reason, many magicians always try to have a quiet word with some member of the audience before the show, asking if he would be kind enough to step up and assist if there seems to be any hold-up at the stage where the magician needs an assistant.

The average spectator naturally feels a certain hesitancy in leaving his or her seat, from which the show can be seen in comfort, and venturing into the bright lights of the platform. There's always the possibility, too, that the magician will play some prank on his volunteer assistant, although this is regarded as being in the worst possible taste.

Many conjurers don't help matters, either, by declaring: "I promise you I won't play any jokes on you, or make you look ridiculous!" The very thought of being made to look ridiculous should never be allowed to enter the spectator's mind.

But it mustn't be thought from all this that the platform show is difficult to stage. Many conjurers, in fact, think that it's easier to put their show on a platform than anywhere else. The magician has his audience just where he wants them—in front of him, and separated from him by several yards' distance and possibly a row of floodlights. He need not worry unduly about anyone seeing his performance from the back. And he has, again, a wide range of tricks from which to choose.

He must always remember, though, that, being at a distance from him, the spectators see him full length, and that every move he makes is going to be fully visible. The question of angles comes up again, but not so acutely as in the case of the club performer. Watching a show on a platform, the spectators at the extreme ends of the front rows sometimes have what could be called a privileged view. The solution to this is for the performer to work farther back on the stage, and to site his tables and apparatus well upstage.

Showy tricks, as well as baffling mysteries, seem to be called for on the platform. Sometimes the magician can combine the two essentials. The Stack of Fishbowls, for example, is exceedingly colourful—and also it's exceedingly baffling. The magician produces a number of large silk squares, apparently from nowhere, and from the midst of them he lifts out a towering pile of goldfish bowls, balanced on top of each other, brimming with water, and containing live goldfish. The resultant show is a splendid one. And if the trick is performed with reasonable skill, the audience haven't the slightest clue as to where the fishbowls could have been concealed before they were brought to light.

On the subject of silk handkerchiefs I could write reams. So few conjurers appreciate the fact that a genuine silk handkerchief of normal size looks tiny and insignificant on the stage. And yet you will see many an amateur magician (and professional ones, too, more's the pity!) proudly produce a dozen or so twelve-inch silks from a box the size of a dog kennel. The silks are often crumpled, and sometimes not too clean.

A silk that's smaller than two feet square should never be used in production tricks. Even then it's not too big. A yard square is nearer the mark. And every silk used should be ironed carefully, at the correct temperature, before being used again.

Ade Duval, the famous American magician, used to present a music-hall act entitled "A Rhapsody in Silk," in the course of which he would literally fill the stage with gorgeous colourful silk squares and banners, even to the very backcloth itself. All these were produced, apparently, from a single small, empty metal tube.

There was mystery—wherever did all the silks come from? There was colour—each silk was specially designed and harmoniously coloured to fit into the general background. There was showmanship—Ade and his charming wife were as surprised as the audience at the enormous production of silks from nowhere. And there was *such* pride in doing a good job of work. Between the first house and the second house, Ade and Mrs. Duval were busy for an hour or more ironing and cleaning the silks used at the previous performance.

If only some of today's magicians, who never press or clean their tiny, tatty silks from one year's end to the next, could appreciate the sheer commercial value of Ade Duval's pride in his work, magic today would be far more colourful and pleasing.

Shall we get back to the subject?

We have to distinguish between what I've called platform magic and the variety shown on a fully equipped theatre stage. The theatre stage can offer us much more in the way of curtain facilities, traps, side-cloths and lighting—all items that may be absent on the modest platform of a church hall or the municipal assembly rooms. If the average church hall has a set of draw curtains, it can be considered well equipped. And if it has a proscenium arch, with the side entrances and exits concealed, it's a thing of wonder.

So the magician booked to show in such a hall should inquire, as soon as he's booked, whether the platform has (*a*) draw curtains, (*b*) side curtains, (*c*) footlights, and (*d*) spotlight.

Without any of these he will be faced with the task of setting his stage in full view of the audience, which is embarrassing indeed. He can get over this setback by having a couple of screens placed at the back and to one side of the stage, and behind them he can set up his apparatus and leave it until his call comes.

But the platform without draw curtains calls for judicious choice of tricks. The magician should be able to carry—or have carried for him—everything in one journey.

A lot of conjurers use a large tray for this purpose. This has advantages, but it is also open to waggishness from the boys in the back row, who are liable to call out: "Chocklitts, Ices, Peanuts, Cigarettes!"

My own preference is for what's known as a roll-on table. This is an enclosed table on wheels, having shelves inside it that carry all the apparatus needed. I have a screen placed as far forward as possible on the platform, and then when my turn comes I simply fold up the screen, and there's my table, all ready set and loaded. If necessary, the table can always be rolled farther forward to the front of the stage.

There should be painted on every platform the motto: "Don't come farther forward than this line!" And the line should be drawn a full three feet behind the footlights. For if the performer stands right on top of the footlights, as so many performers *do* stand, his face is in darkness, and the upward lighting obscures much of what he's doing. It's a great temptation, this urge to crowd on top of the footlights, but to do so ruins one's performance.

On a platform equipped with adequate curtains, the magician can stage not only tricks but big-scale illusions—provided that they don't need trap-doors or cables lowered from the flies. He can prepare the stage beforehand. He can run fine black threads across the stage if he wishes. He can drive tacks into the battens at the sides. He can—if he has access to the stage before the show—do almost anything he wishes that doesn't conflict with the ideas of the owners of the hall.

But, best of all, he can make a dignified entry when his cue comes, for all his equipment will have been placed on the platform behind the decent obscurity of the front curtain.

Moreover, he can make an equally dignified exit after his curtain call. The first time he does so he will almost certainly ruin the dignity of his curtain call by losing the opening of the curtains. He will fumble madly for the edge of the curtain so that he may get off the platform and retire once more to his own private life. But the second time he takes a curtain call he will surely remember to keep a light hold of the edge of the outer curtain—

usually the right-hand one—so that he may open it gracefully after he's taken his bow, and retire successfully. When you see an entertainer holding the edge of the curtain as he takes his bow before the tabs, you may now know that he isn't simply finding something for his hand to do. He's making sure he can find his way off the stage.

Having achieved the glory of working on the assembly rooms platform, the magician will, let's hope, know where everything is to go on that platform, and will see to it that everything *does* go there. It's not sufficient to murmur foolishly: "It'll be all right on the night." It hardly ever is all right on the night, unless there have been thorough rehearsals. And rehearsals don't only mean practising the tricks. They also mean going through the performance in private *exactly* as it will be gone through in public. This applies, of course, to any kind of magic. The close-up trickster must take these same precautions, just as the pocket-trick man and the floor-show entertainer must.

The conjurer on the platform must know where to turn to pick a thing up and to lay it down. He must know exactly where his tables are going to be, so that he could find them without looking. The best way to do this is to perform the whole show beforehand, with tables, chairs, and all apparatus placed exactly as they'll be sited on stage. That way, there should be little risk of the enthusiastic conjurer turning smartly to his table, loaded with props—and knocking the lot over. It often happens, and it often means the end of *that* show.

A word, please, about those eager voluntary helpers backstage. One of them will offer to carry your table on to the stage for you.
DON'T LET HIM TOUCH IT!
He'll almost surely place it on the stage back to front or sideways—that is, if he succeeds in getting up the steps to the stage without dropping everything.

In fact, don't let anyone touch *anything* of yours behind the scenes. If you do allow your apparatus to be handled, you'll certainly find that your carefully stacked pack of cards has been shuffled, your hidden thread broken, your trick slates turned upside down, and your rabbit suffocated. You deserve all that happens to you—and it *will* happen!—if you let people handle your apparatus before a show.

The bigger the platform, the bigger the hall, as a rule. And the bigger the hall, the bigger the audience. That means that the tricks performed must be on a more generous scale. Card tricks, now: performing in a big hall means that most card tricks are OUT. People at the back of the hall can't tell one card from another. But card tricks in which the cards are merely used as conveniently shaped *articles*, instead of playing cards, are quite in order.

The famous old Cards Across—often called the Twenty Card Trick, the Thirty Card Trick, and by lots of other names—is safe enough. In this one, two spectators each have, say, ten cards. By some mysterious means, the conjurer manages to make three or four cards pass from one packet, held by one spectator, to the other packet, in the possession of the other spectator. The cards, you see, are used merely as objects, and not as playing cards. Their values don't matter. Nobody has to look at a card and identify it.

Coin tricks, save for the Miser's Dream and its variants, in which the magician catches many silver coins from the air, are only for the specialist showman when it comes to showing them on a platform in a large hall. Coins are even smaller than cards, and it takes a deuce of a lot of them to make anything of a show.

I once saw a magician do a trick with matches on a stage. When the trick was over, he wondered why nobody applauded.

All in all, there's much to be learnt about performing on a stage. But it must be learnt by experience. Fortunately, the experience is usually quickly acquired, and it's a pleasant form of learning.

When it comes to cash outlay, the club performer and the platform magician probably invest more in their props than any other amateur or semi-professional entertainer. The club performer may stage an excellent show at little cost if his sleight of hand is good. But if he finds this branch of his art difficult, he must buy tricks that don't demand sleight of hand. They can be expensive. To buy good apparatus for performing half a dozen good tricks could cost £10, at a very reasonable estimate. True, one can buy cheap tricks, but a programme full of them looks cheap.

Tricks that will look well on a platform, apart from those performed by sheer sleight of hand, can cost anything from a modest five shillings to many pounds. If the novice has £10 or £15 to spend, he can build up a programme of six or eight reasonably good tricks that could make a nice show. Mind you, if twice or three times that amount can be spent, the show could be that much more varied.

For example, if you simply must catch a chosen card on the point of a sword, that sword will cost you between £3 and £5—more, if made to your own specification.

Apart from tricks, the platform magician needs a table. To use a card table belonging to the hall neither looks good nor brings much confidence. They one and all seem to be cursed with faulty catches, and will *always* collapse when touched. So the conjurer should carry his own table or tables with him. These may vary from a neat, small affair that can be taken to pieces and carried in an attaché case to the more cumbersome—but good-looking and useful—roll-on table, which needs a car to carry it, even in its folded state.

Every magician seems to start out on his magical career with what he fondly believes to be the ideal table. This is a horrible contraption made from the folding tripod legs of an old music-stand, and its top is draped with black velvet, criss-crossed with gold braid or tape. Such tables went out with the coming of the steam engine. Please, *please*, don't use a table made from an old music-stand and draped in black velvet.

The magical dealers sell good neat collapsible tables that are much more reliable—and much more beautiful to look at. Such a table could cost from £5 upwards for a good one. One dealer markets an elaborate and cleverly designed folding table that collapses into a suitcase, in which all the apparatus can be carried. That's more money still.

Let's say that you want to put on a pretty ambitious show on your local stage. If you'd like to saw a lady in half, it may cost you as little as £25, or as much as ten times that amount.

If you then aspire to make your lady assistant float in the air—*really* float, not merely remain uncertainly suspended for a few seconds—then you'd better start thinking in terms of £200. It may surprise you to learn that the piece of machinery you'll need for this needn't be the only expense. You may need to have special curtains made for the illusion.

Very well. You don't want to saw a lady in half, and you don't want to spend all that money on making her airborne. You'll settle for the Linking Rings (say £3 a set), the Twenty Card Trick (three shillings a pack), the Cups and Balls (say £2), the Cut and Restored Rope Trick (say ten shillings), and a good showy climax, producing a dozen yard-square silks from somewhere or other (thirty-five shillings each for the silks and perhaps £3 for the whatever-it-is to produce them from). You'll need a table, too, so let's add £5 for that.

My goodness! You've spent more than £35! Where's the money gone? Why, it's gone on five tricks and a table. Remember?

But remember this, as well: having got the tricks, you will need several months in which to learn how to perform them and present them properly.

I wish every organiser of an entertainment would bear this in mind whenever he wonders whether that magician he'd like to book is worth as much as five guineas for his show.

Ah well! If you're bent on being a magician, you won't let a little thing like money stand in your way.

CHAPTER FOUR

A MINDREADER, EH?

IN the previous chapter I only discussed what might be called the varying sizes of packages in which magic comes, from the tiny pocket trick to the stage illusion. I haven't yet mentioned the varying styles of magic. Usually, you can break magic down into three styles: orthodox magic (tricks and illusions), mental magic (mindreading, predictions, etc.), and sensational magic (fire-walking, escapes, etc.).

It is with orthodox magic that the average spectator is most familiar, because this is the type most practised, and consequently he sees more of it, and sees it more often. Mental magic isn't so familiar to him, because there are fewer practitioners of it on a professional scale.

Mental magic has one unique quality: it *could* be a genuine phenomenon. At least, that's the popular theory with many intelligent spectators. Whereas they know that the orthodox conjurer is employing trickery, they are seldom quite sure, at the bottom of their minds, about the expert mentalist.

For that reason, I don't think it's good showmanship to include a straight-faced mental effect in a programme of ordinary conjuring. I also believe that the audience should be left to work out for themselves the question: "Is it genuine?" The mentalist, to be strictly ethical, should make no claim to the possession of supernormal powers, but neither should be blandly inform the audience that it's all a trick. Besides—*it isn't all a trick!*

The Piddingtons, those extremely baffling mentalists, had the best formula, when they used to leave the audience with their catch-line: "You are the judges!"

The mentalist is supposed to be a man who can read minds, plant his own thoughts in other people's minds, predict what will happen in the future, and read what has happened in the past.

That being so, he must be a pretty smart fellow, the audience will agree. And if he's so smart, he won't need a lot of tricked apparatus, such as they've seen used by conjurers. The minute the spectators see a recognised piece of conjuring apparatus, they know, to their own complete satisfaction, that the

35

mentalist is a conjurer. And they're a bit sorry about that, for they'd been hoping he was a mindreader!

There are two kinds of mental performance: the one in which the performer works alone, and the one in which a partner is used. Maurice Fogel—"The Amazing Mr. Fogel"—is a leading example of the former. The Piddingtons are a recent brilliant example of the latter.

Speaking generally, the solo performer has the harder task. He's entirely alone up there on the stage, and all his wonders must be accomplished entirely by his own efforts. That's understandable, but there's another difficulty: he may only use those effects which a single-handed mentalist could naturally be expected to use—*if he were genuine*. Once he succeeds in presenting the flagrantly impossible, he will be written off as a fraud in the minds of the otherwise credulous audience.

For example, everybody is familiar with the two-person act in which the performer conveys his thoughts to his assistant. But imagine for a moment that a solo performer did the same thing, obtaining the same lightning, snappy answers from a member of the audience. Would it seem feasible? Of course it wouldn't. The audience would straightway spot the assisting spectator as a confederate. Magicians refer to such a confederate as a stooge.

And so the solo performer must not infringe the bounds of possibility or credibility.

The two-person act, however, is permitted much more latitude, because here the audience are conditioned to believe that the performer can transmit his thoughts to his assistant through long practice, and because his assistant is perhaps psychic.

So the solo mentalist may bring off the most sublime miracles of telepathy, prediction and divination so long as he doesn't strain the audience's credibility too far. The dividing line between belief and ridicule is a very fine one. And the mentalist must know *exactly* how near that dividing line he may go. Most amateur mentalists step over it a dozen times in the performance of one trick because they have not explored their own limitations.

Fogel, now, gets away with the most astounding feats, simply because he has the personality that impresses the spectators with his power. If Maurice Fogel were a timid, half-hearted magician, who would credit his mystic powers? As it is, he possesses, and makes the most of, a high-powered personality and a faultless appearance.

I have sat in the stalls and watched Fogel perform an apparent miracle by the simplest and boldest means. What's more, I've known for certain what means he was employing—and yet I've been as amazed as the rest of the audience. The mentalist watching Fogel may say to himself: "He could only do that by using a billet switch. And yet he *can't* be using a billet switch."

That's showmanship of the highest degree.

But Fogel would never, never, trespass across the boundary between credibility and incredibility. It would be the easiest thing in the world for him to incorporate into his programme some item that would surpass any wonder the spectators had seen before, by crossing the border of credibility. But you will never find Fogel doing that.

The expert mentalist, you will find, *is* a mentalist. In other words, he *has* powers that few other people possess. But those powers are by no means supernatural or supernormal. Some—indeed most—mentalists are masters of one or other of the well-known memory systems. Many of them are lightning calculators of high ability. Others are blessed with unusually keen eyesight and sharp perception. All the good ones are practised experts in psychology, and from experience can divine the track of a person's thoughts. They will direct those thoughts into their own channel by subtle suggestion, so that the spectator unwittingly thinks what the mentalist *wants* him to think.

You may prove this easily. In one trick I perform, I ask a spectator—any spectator—to think of a card, and then to announce the name of the card he is thinking of. I then ask the rest of the audience: "Did anyone else think of the same card?" Invariably, in an audience of any size, several people hold up their hands. Whereupon I say: "*You*, then, have read this gentleman's [the spectator's] mind, too!"

How, you may ask, do other people come to think of the same card? The answer is that the laws of probability are at work. A list is available to magicians showing the principal cards of which people will think first. This has been compiled after thousands of experiments. Yes, the Ace of Spades and the King of Hearts come high on the list. In other words, when asked to name a card, the average person *only has a limited choice*. If he is given time to think, he may name the Three of Diamonds, for example. But if he is hurried, he will name one that springs more easily to his mind. And if fifty people are asked to write the name of the first card that comes to their mind, you will find that the majority have shared the Ace of Spades, the King of Diamonds, and the Queen of Hearts.

But, in a large audience, when the mentalist asks "Quickly, please, quickly!" for the name of a card, it doesn't matter how long the spectators take to think it over. *They only have fifty-two cards to choose from.* And so, if there are 520 people in the audience, one card will be named *at least ten times*.

That may give a false impression, and you may think that this mentalism is easier than it really is. It isn't, you know. First of all, even for the "easy" items such as the one I've just mentioned, *you have to know the principle*.

And if you think it's going to be easy, just try that popular feat, the

Giant Memory (in which the mentalist remembers perfectly a long, complicated list of miscellaneous objects), without knowing the principle. If you can name five out of twenty of the complex objects usually named, you are doing well. But if you have the principle, you will remember every one perfectly, and be able to recite the list backwards or forwards.

Where will you find the principle? Well, if you study the Pelman System you will learn something of the method used. If you subscribe to the Roth Memory System you will be able to perform the Giant Memory. "Ah!" you may say, "it's not worth the trouble!" Neither is it—unless you intend to be a convincing mentalist.

When you are planning some event ahead, how often do you ask yourself: "Now what day will September 13th fall on next year?" You look at the calendar or your pocket diary, and there is the information you need.

But the expert mentalist will be able to tell you in two seconds what day *any* date—in *any* year, back or forward—will fall upon. Could you do that? I'm sure you couldn't—unless you knew the principle involved. And even if you had read the system thoroughly, I feel quite sure that you would be considerably dismayed at the amount of memorising called for even to learn the formula used in the "Day for any date" feat.

When I first studied this feat, I tried it on a friend who is something of an historian. He at once asked: "What day did they fight the Battle of Waterloo?" My calculations showed the day to be a Sunday, which my friend dismissed with scorn. It was weeks later when I was able to check that date. The Battle of Waterloo—June 18th, 1815—*was* fought on a Sunday.

Since then, I have often given the day for a particular date and been told I'm wrong. But a little checking proves that calculation beats memory nine times out of ten. I have also found that many people *do not know* the day they call for. This is an interesting sidelight on human nature. One finds it rather more often than one should, when performing mentalism. A person is asked, say, to think of a name. The mentalist then tells him the name he has thought of. The spectator is quite liable to deny the name offered, and to say he thought of something else.

It is for this reason that the mentalist insists on such thoughts being written down. When they are committed to paper, you see, he has a check by which he can verify his correctness—or otherwise!—for the rest of the audience.

There is one more reason why the mentalist demands written proof in this manner. But I am not at liberty to disclose that reason!

I mentioned the inadvisability of the use of conjuring apparatus by the mentalist. The reason should be obvious, but, alas! it isn't. Consider this: a mentalist demonstrates mindreading, and uses a recognisable piece of magical apparatus, such as a Changing Bag, that curious object which is only seen on the conjurer's stage and in churches. (And, gentle reader, if you do not know what a Changing Bag is, I will tell you that it's a bag which changes things. If you see one in church, that's not a Changing Bag; it's a collection bag.)

There is really little need for the Changing Bag in any performance, orthodox or not, but the spectators, although they know well what the thing's for, will patiently put up with it in the normal conjuring performance. In the mentalist's show, however, they will smile knowingly, for they know just what a Changing Bag is, and what it does.

Now imagine that the mentalist hasn't got a Changing Bag. But he has access to a score or more of useful devices that will exchange one thing for another, each quite normal in appearance—which the Changing Bag is not. So he decides to use, let's say, a packet of envelopes to perform what's known as the envelope switch. There! You didn't even guess he was going to exchange an envelope, did you?

What's more normal than a packet of envelopes in the hand when envelopes are required? Who'd suspect that they might be tricked in any way? And, not suspecting, aren't the spectators more likely to accept the wonders of the mentalist who, cunning fellow, is using nothing but normal, everyday articles in his show?

It's one thing (though not necessarily a good thing) to have the backcloth splattered with sequin question marks, and curtains and banners bearing the inscription: "The Great Gizmo, World's Master Mentalist," and it's another thing entirely to have the stage cluttered with red-and-gold boxes, chromium-plated tubes, velvet-draped tables and the like. The former may at least be in keeping with the mentalist's performance, but the latter is only consonant with the stage display of the apparatus conjurer.

So if we're going to be mindreaders, let's use the simplest, most ordinary things. Writing pads are more normal than slates in these days, so let's try, with a writing pad, to get the same effects that the old mindreaders used to get with their Spirit Slates. Anyway, if we must use a slate, let's make an excuse for it, or find a reason for it. What reason? Why—it's so much easier to see a large slate than a writing pad from the back seats of a large hall. But if we're going to do close-up work, let's discard slates. Spectators at close quarters can see pencil writing on a pad quite plainly.

It's amazing how much faking can be done to the ordinary items of everyday life. You simply wouldn't believe, for instance, the number of ways—imperceptible ways, too—in which an ordinary envelope can be prepared. And I would never dream of telling you! Pencils, pens, pads of paper, even single sheets of paper, can be prepared so subtly for the mindreader's secret purposes that, examine them how you will, you would never detect the manner or the purpose of their preparation.

How's your memory? Unless it's good, I wouldn't advise you to take up mentalism. A mindreader has to keep several jumps ahead of his audience. Accordingly, he must remember every relevant word for later repetition when necessary. He must be able to memorise at a glance a hand of cards. He must be able to commit to memory a written message only partly glimpsed in one split second. He should, too, be able when challenged to remember such oddments of information as motor-car numbers, telephone numbers, dates, and scraps of useful information.

Here's an instance of how memory and general knowledge can help the mindreader. I once had to build up on a single word. That means that I knew *one word* that was in the spectator's mind, and from it I had to give him quite a long story. That one word was "Blackpool."

This is what I said:

"I'm getting an impression of height—height, with some figures attached to it. The figures seem to be 500—no, more than that—520 feet. That's odd. What could 520 feet mean? Now there are words—'520 feet with the flagpole.' Tell me, does this mean anything to you? It doesn't seem to make much sense to me! It *does* mean something to you? I'm glad of that! Now let's go on: there's a high building—no, not a building; it's made of metal—with a flagpole on it. The Eiffel Tower? No. It's nearer home than that. Blackpool Tower—YES! Blackpool Tower. Were you thinking of Blackpool Tower?"

The person nodded delightedly. But really, you know, he *wasn't* thinking of Blackpool Tower; he was thinking of the town of Blackpool. I'd *led* him to think of Blackpool Tower.

And the height of Blackpool Tower—520 feet with flagpole—is pretty well known to anyone who's visited Blackpool. The Tower Company like to tell the visitors how high they've soared in the lift up the Tower. I knew the height of the Tower. From that it was possible to build the rest—which was pure padding!

If the word in the spectator's mind had been "Salisbury" I'd have had another odd fact to build on—Salisbury has the highest cathedral spire in the country. If the word had been Doncaster I'd have built up on the race meetings held there. A little titbit of knowledge about as many places as possible can be invaluable to the mindreader.

Another useful asset is the ability to place accents. It creates a tremendous impression if the mentalist can tell a person what town he comes from. I can place accents moderately well for Lancashire and Yorkshire and the Midlands, and I do find that the spectator who is given a short word-picture of his home town is greatly impressed. Although he hasn't mentioned or written the name of his home town, the mindreader knows it! There's magic for you! And it becomes even more magical when the mindreader deliberately avoids mentioning the town *by name*, but simply describes a few outstanding features of it.

Then, it savours of genuine mindreading.

And it isn't a trick, in the usual sense of the word. It's the straightforward use of powers that anyone already has, or could cultivate, combined with psychology. The psychology lies in omitting the *name* of the town.

Generally, as you will have gathered, the mindreader's chief asset is subtlety rather than sleight of hand, psychology rather than apparatus. But it can be a costly business.

The mentalist—the *good* mentalist—can stage a fine performance at little more than the cost of a Swami Gimmick (half a crown) and a few pencils and note pads. If he is more ambitious in his spending, he can use costly electronic equipment to the value of hundreds of pounds.

The scope of the mentalist is only limited by his personality. If he can convince people that his wonders *could* be genuine phenomena (without saying so in as many words, of course), then he can go far as a mindreader. But if he is of hesitant personality, vague in presentation, unsure of himself, he had better buy himself some conjurer's apparatus and become an orthodox magician.

One wishes that this was generally appreciated, but, more's the pity, it isn't. You will see and hear would-be mindreaders whose knowledge of English is faulty, and who talk of "fenomenums" instead of phenomena. You will hear them assure you that "I've wrote it before you done it." You will see them in flowing velvet capes and top hat and tails—but wearing a black tie and soft collar. You'll see them writing their predictions with stubby bits of chewed pencil. (Watch Fogel and see the brilliant play he makes with his large white pencil!) You'll see them going through their performance as if they'd been *condemned* to be mindreaders, instead of putting it over as though they delighted in sharing their "unique" powers with their friends, the spectators.

Why do they do this?

The answer is that they like performing better than the spectators like watching them perform. These are the magical bores, akin to the "Take a card, look at it, remember it, put it back in the pack and shuffle it" man. These are the sad and sorry brethren of the trickster brigade, who "do tricks" instead of entertaining with magic.

Before we leave the mindreaders, let's take a side glance at some kindred branches of magic.

Hypnotism. Now there's a fascinating thing! But is it entertainment?

And—let's whisper this—is it always genuine? Because to fake a hypnotic presentation requires the use of stooges, and ethically that's bad. The genuine hypnotist—and make no mistake, there are lots of them—needs no stooges. He can, and will, hypnotise most of those who step up on the platform for the purpose.

How?

One answer is that the volunteer assistants are already half conditioned before they enter the theatre. Take a look at the photographic display advertising a hypnotist's performance. See the "subjects" lined up there in the publicity pictures, hypnotised into believing they are six years old, believing they are rowing boats, believing they are conducting orchestras, believing they are doing one or other of the absurd things the hypnotist wishes them to perform. These subjects look pretty convincing, don't they? He must be a powerful hypnotist, mustn't he?

There! Now *you're* half conditioned!

In other words, if you believe the hypnotist can hypnotise you—he can! And so before you've entered the hall you are half-way to being convinced that he could hypnotise *you*. To make quite sure, you may want to step up to the platform and test him for yourself. If you do this, you'll probably miss half the show, for you may soon be fast asleep on the stage. *You* will be giving the show you've paid to see.

Have you ever sat in a bus or a train and seen somebody yawn? Of course you have—and you've yawned yourself. You couldn't help wanting to yawn, though you don't know why. Have you ever seen somebody sucking a lemon, and felt your own mouth start to water? These are two elementary reactions to the power of suggestion. The hypnotist carries the power of suggestion much farther than that, because he instils complete confidence in you. If he tells you that you cannot feel a pin driven through your flesh, and you have such complete confidence, you will *not* feel that pin.

One simple and convincing test which some hypnotists apply in order to find the suggestibility of their audiences is this: the hypnotist tells the spectators that there are ants in the hall. Everybody knows that an insect crawling on the skin can cause intense itching. Within seconds, many spectators are scratching themselves. They *believe* that they have ants crawling on them. This is a crude test indeed. But it works. By noting those spectators who are scratching, the hypnotist recognises the ones who are—to coin a word—hypnotisable.

Since the law was amended with respect to hypnotism, one does not see so many hypnotists performing in theatres. But many amateur magicians rather fancy their powers as hypnotists, and are usually eager to try their powers on any willing subject.

The advice of expert hypnotists is—DON'T LET AN AMATEUR ATTEMPT TO HYPNOTISE YOU! It is really so easy to hypnotise a person that many, many people are potential hypnotists if they did but know it. Once they know it, they are anxious to try it out. But the danger lies in the fact that most of them don't know what they are doing, and the after-effects of amateur hypnotism can be harmful.

It is comparatively easy to persuade a person suffering from mild pain that the pain doesn't exist. Combined with some knowledge of the manipulation of nerves and muscles, it is simpler still to alleviate pain. Severe toothache can be abated in seconds by pressure on the facial nerves at the right spot. BUT THE CAUSE OF THE TOOTHACHE IS STILL THERE.

And it will remain there if the pain—Nature's signal that something's wrong—is destroyed. The result will be a tooth that is allowed to decay painlessly without the correct dental treatment.

So it seems logical that the cause of the pain should be treated, rather than the pain itself. It is for this reason that the amateur hypnotist is a dangerous fellow. He will gladly demonstrate his powers to take away pain, while leaving the cause there. Apart from this aspect of his performance, there are other, even more dangerous results possible. But this book is no place for a discussion of the ethical rights and wrongs of hypnotism.

Let's leave the subject at this: the amateur hypnotist should be discouraged from practising upon *anybody*.

And after all—is hypnotism in public *really* entertaining?

The mentalist may, of course, use "hypnotism" as an explanation of his powers. But it isn't the true explanation.

We've already taken a glance at the lightning calculator, who is another exponent of mentalism. His brand of mind magic, though, is genuine. Mind you, he uses short cuts and secret mathematical formulæ, but without any other aid he is able to perform wonders of mental arithmetic.

My friend Frederick Barlow, in his book *Mental Prodigies*, has reviewed this aspect of mentalism thoroughly, and makes it plain that there are people who are specially disposed to this complex art. Calculating boys, always regarded as phenomena, are truly a mystery. They lose their powers, often, when they grow up, and the question of how they acquired their youthful calculating powers remains an unsolved problem.

But for such comparatively simple experiments as rapid multiplication, the extraction of square roots and cube roots, calendar calculations and the like, there are recognised methods. These methods, though, demand as much concentration to learn as do the final sums which result from them.

I have already mentioned such a method, for calendar calculation, which I use. This method was passed to me by Mr. Barlow, and for a long time I believed that he and I and the originator (who is a well-known magician in the Midlands) were the only three people using this method. But when I met Wim Klein, the Dutch calculating prodigy, I learned that he too had worked out an almost exactly similar method. We compared notes, and Klein was as surprised as I was to find that the "secret" was shared by someone else.

After that, whenever we met, instead of exchanging the normal greetings, we would fire at each other test problems in calendar calculation!

I have often wondered why some of the lightning calculators' mathematical formulæ are not taught in schools, where, it seems, children still learn their figures the hard way.

The memory experts: how do they perform their incredible feats of mental magic?—for true mental magic it is.

In the case of most of them, their powers are as mysterious as are those of the calculating boys. There are, of course, systems for memorising lists of names and numbers, but the true expert is not content with such matters.

Jimmy Green, for instance, under his stage name of Michael Shaw, baffled the experts of the Magic Circle for years—and, for the matter of that, still has them baffled. Green used to perform the incredible task of memorising —*word by word and figure by figure*—the whole of the contents of the London Bradshaw's Railway Time-table, the A.B.C. Railway Time-table, and the London Passenger Transport Guide. He could tell you in a flash what bus went where, as well as outlining the railway services over the whole of the Kingdom, complete with oddments of information such as "Restaurant car on Tuesdays and Thursdays" and "Not stopping at Little Trembling except on Fridays."

This, to me, is true magic.

I am as convinced as I can be that Jimmy Green used no artificial aids to memory, in the form of prompters, written or spoken. I have tested his amazing powers in private and have stood a few feet from him, in the wings, as he performed his remarkable act on the stage. All he needs is Jimmy Green on the platform and the time-tables in the audience as a check.

Jimmy Green has now more or less retired from the stage—although still a young man—and lives a peaceful life in Devonshire, where lobster pots and boating are more important to him than the 6.15 to Market Harborough (6.21 on Sundays). I often wonder whether he retains his powers, which have never yet, to my knowledge, been fully explained.

Leslie Welch, "The Memory Man," is still performing his miracles on the stage, of course, and delighting audiences of sportsmen on the radio. In Welch's case, here is a man with a consuming interest in sport, and with application and diligence he has been able to commit to memory all the dates, names and fixtures that interest him—and the rest of the sporting world.

Again an example of true magic, beside which the modest manipulations and cunning devices of the conjurer are like children's toys.

Not all the mental wizards are on the stage. In Alexandria, Egypt, there used to be a blind beggar who sat by the dusty roadside in the Rue Fouad. For a small coin he would tell you the time—to within a minute each way. That may not seem unusual, but remember this: the old man was totally and completely blind, and indeed, had no eyes whatsoever. He could not, therefore, see a watch or clock, and he certainly possessed no such thing as a Braille watch. I have checked on his powers dozens of times when I lived in Alexandria, and never once was he more than a minute out in his decision.

The odd thing was that nobody thought anything of this amazing demonstration, and took it as a matter of course.

The only clue I ever found to these uncanny powers was the fact that the old man constantly rocked from side to side. He may have calculated the passage of time by the number of movements—but how could he be sure that each movement was of exactly the right duration?

Many ex-soldiers will remember "The Minute Man," as the old Arab was called.

I leave the problem of his weird powers with you. How did he do it? I don't know. Do you?

Have you ever had your weight guessed on a fairground? If the man guessed your weight and the weights of all your friends accurately, thus taking your money as payment, you may be sure it was done by a simple trick. The man was writing your weight on the card secretly, after you had told him your weight.

Here is the procedure: the man looks you over, and writes on a card: "Your weight is . . ." He leaves the figure blank. You do not see what he has written—yet. He then says: "I have written your exact weight on this card. Will you tell us how much you weigh?" You tell him, and then he writes in the figure. No, of course, you don't see him do it. Why not? Take a close look at the man's left thumb. You'll find the answer there . . .

The man who really guesses your weight, without trickery, does so by looking you over and estimating, by long practice, just what you weigh. You, too, can learn to do this merely by trial and error until you get the hang of it.

If ever you feel tempted to visit a fortune-teller, you may get a surprise. She (or sometimes he) will tell you an amazing amount about yourself. Usually, this is done by keen observation, but in the case of women clients it is made easier by the subject's talkative habits. An odd "Yes, indeed," or a shake of the head—maybe unconsciously done—will tell the astute fortune-teller a lot.

You'll often find, while the fortune-teller is holding your hand, palm upwards, that she is not looking at the palm, but at your face, judging your reactions from your expressions as her tale is told. *You* are looking at your palm, though, and so don't see that she is watching your facial reactions. Next time you have your palm read, say nothing, wear no jewellery (for such things tell their own tale), write nothing—either on paper or slate— and *watch the fortune-teller's eyes.*

Of course, you may well come away disappointed, unless you are of the type that is content to receive a message—yet to be proved correct—about the future.

An even less reputable distant cousin of the mentalist is the fraudulent spiritualist medium. These people rely entirely on the extreme credulity of their victims, allied with the use of every possible conjurer's device that they can operate unperceived.

I have nothing to say about such harpies beyond KEEP AWAY FROM THEM.

But the fortune-teller and the fake medium are only the remotest kin— although they use many of his methods—of the mentalist whose magic is designed to *entertain*. Whereas they practise their squalid art solely for as much money as they can get out of their victims, the mental magician aims to bring pleasure to his spectators. He brings them mystery as well, but his prime aim is to entertain.

And that should be the aim of every magician, whether he uses his alert mind, ingenious mechanical devices, or pure sleight of hand.

CHAPTER FIVE

A FULL HAND OF CLUBS

IF you live in London, you may one day see a man wearing in his buttonhole a small badge showing the Ace of Clubs on a white background. And if ever you're in the neighbourhood of Conway Hall, Red Lion Square, on a Friday evening, you'll see a score or more of such badges.

For Conway Hall is the meeting place of members of the London Society of Magicians, and the Ace of Clubs is the badge they wear.

Great Britain has something like seventy or more magical societies. London alone has half a dozen, quite apart from the Magic Circle, and there are probably another half-dozen or so in the Home Counties. And yet it's surprising how many keen amateur magicians know nothing of their local magical society. The list of such societies included in this book may help to introduce the "lone wolf" conjurer to his fellow magicians.

And—getting back to our subject—if you live in London, you might do much worse than contact the London Society of Magicians. This is one of the younger societies, having been founded in 1941, but its youth doesn't mean that it hasn't acquired maturity yet.

How do you join a magical society?

Well, taking the L.S.M. as an example, you'll need to be eighteen years of age at least, and must be prepared to show that your interest in magic is more than idle curiosity. If you don't feel that your interest is strong enough to justify your applying for full membership, you can become an associate member for a very modest fee, which will entitle you to attend the Society's shows as well as all open meetings and general meetings.

How much does it cost?

The L.S.M., which is a fair example of the more important "localised" societies, will ask you for a five-shilling entrance fee and a guinea-and-a-half yearly subscription. Associate membership calls for an annual subscription of ten shillings.

In most magical societies you'll need to find a proposer and a seconder for you, but the secretary will usually be glad to introduce you to some members for this purpose.

The L.S.M. meets once a week, and has a student section for magicians between fourteen and seventeen years of age, who hold their meetings once a fortnight. Most provincial societies meet once a fortnight, and many of them have junior sections.

Sometimes these juniors show a mild interest in tricks, rather than magic, and sometimes such members drift in and out of one society after another. But most younger members stay in and become confirmed magical addicts— and, frequently, first-class entertainers. One such young magician who springs to mind is Robert Solbé, of the Nottingham Guild of Magicians. Robert, who is still under twenty years of age, joined the Nottingham Guild as a schoolboy. At first, his style was aggressive, as though he wished to cover up a natural nervousness in performing before older people. Then, when a year or two's experience had abated what nerves he might have had, he developed a delightfully witty style which won him television broadcasts and professional engagements *while he was still at school.*

You'll find a number of such youthful wizards among the members of the London Society of Magicians. Before they're out of their teens they have developed an uncanny ability for sleight of hand, and by the time they're ten years older they're reputable entertainers making useful guineas by performing in public.

But it's not only for personal gain that the magicians' clubs exist. Most of them do excellent work for charity. Indeed, one of the aims of the L.S.M. is the raising of funds for charity by means of the magical entertainments they hold. The same applies to most, if not all, of the magicians' clubs throughout the country. Many of them count charitable work as their prime aim, and their members lend their talents freely year by year to aid their local deserving causes.

On this subject, it's pleasant to think that entertainers in general (and, I often think, magicians in particular) are among the world's greatest givers. If it isn't money that they give, it's their ability to entertain. Some years ago, while living in Sidcup, Kent, I was asked to organise an entertainment in aid of the Soldiers', Sailors' and Airmen's Families Association. A little hesitantly, I approached Francis White, then secretary of the Magic Circle, and asked if he thought one or two members might be able to come along and do a show. Within minutes of the request, I had a list of ten first-class magicians anxious to help. The result was that the curtain rang up some days later on a bill that would have cost more than £100 if each magician had been paid his normal fee. And the charity concerned netted several hundred pounds for its funds, thanks to the innate generosity and anxiety to help displayed by the artistes, some of whom travelled many miles to be present.

Some magical societies devote a great deal of time and patient work to an annual charitable effort, putting on their show for a week at a time at their local theatre. Most are freely "on call" to local charitable organisers, either as individuals or as a concerted programme.

Apart from the charitable aspect, this is a good thing for the members of the societies. It affords a fine opportunity for their younger members to perform in front of a big audience, and that's an opportunity they might not otherwise get.

Leaving aside the question of doing good for others, the magicians' clubs are of great value to their members by reason of the pool of experience that's available to each member.

Most magicians get their start by acquiring a book of tricks. According to the nature of the book, they develop more or less rapidly as conjurers. But until they can compare notes with other, and more experienced, conjurers, they find that advancement is slow. There are exceptions, though.

I remember that a young magician—still a schoolboy—was brought as a visitor to the Magic Circle once. He'd seen stage magicians, and had decided to take up conjuring as a hobby. But—*he didn't know how to start*. He didn't know that books on the subject were available, or that there were shops dealing in magical tricks and secrets. And so he devoted many months to evolving his own techniques at sleight of hand. The result was that when he came down to the Magic Circle clubroom, he completely and utterly baffled the members with the few card moves he had worked out for himself. Thinking along completely original lines, he had developed new sleights, new misdirection, new effects, which were quite unknown to the experienced magicians.

I often think that it's a pity this young conjurer ever learned that there were already accepted techniques of magic! If he'd pursued his own way for a few more years, he'd have originated a completely new art of magic.

But such diligent students are rare indeed. Most of us started by buying a book on card tricks, and steadily working on it until we were as near perfect as solitary practice could make us. Then we came to a halt, until we fell in with another magician who had a few ideas to swop. After that we progressed fast, and met other conjurers, exchanging still more ideas, and absorbing still more polished technique.

And so the magicians' clubs came into existence.

Wherever you go in Great Britain, you'll find these little assemblies of magicians, meeting regularly, pooling their ideas, criticising each other's performance, and generally helping each other.

Despite this atmosphere of mutual help, though, some cynics believe in keeping one's better effects to oneself. "Pirates!" they whisper confidingly. "They'll pinch your best stuff if you let them see it!"

Unfortunately, that's true to a certain extent. Many clubs seem to have one or two members who attend to see what the other fellow has that's good, rather than to offer anything themselves. And, alas! these pirates are usually ingenious fellows who can see through the secret of a trick and make it up for themselves. Give them an idea and they'll produce a trick. So you'll find that many prominent members of the magicians' clubs will do one of two things: either they'll specialise on a particular branch of sleight of hand that can only be copied after long and diligent practice (and the pirates don't often care for long practice!), or else they'll keep their best mysteries only for performance to a lay audience.

In my own case, I have one or two mental mysteries that I wouldn't care to show to strange magicians. Most of them depend upon cultivated feats of memory and calculation, which usually cannot be duplicated by trick methods, but still . . . I always have the thought in my mind that some day someone *might* copy one of these mysteries by means of trickery.

Apart from this, members of magician's clubs are generous in contributing their knowledge to aid their fellow members. The stock tricks and sleights are readily available to the less experienced members, who progress quickly by seeing the actual methods of performing these mysteries.

One of the features of all magical clubs, indeed, is a syllabus of lectures, in the course of which specialists in one magical subject or another patiently and fully disclose style, technique and method. This is invaluable to any magician. Personal instruction can do in ten minutes what a book cannot do in ten years.

And of course the great feature of magical clubs is the good fellowship they afford. Magicians are (I record the fact with all due modesty!) pretty intelligent fellows, whatever their calling in life. So one gets a clear-cut cross-section of intelligent, informed opinion on many aspects of life when one joins a magical club. In one club to which I had the privilege of belonging in the provinces, our members numbered several business executives, a colonel in the Army, an expert textile draughtsman, a musician, a school teacher, a bank official, two very highly placed civil servants, a printer, a grocer, an hotel manager, a farmer, a bookmaker and many others. Each was an expert in his own particular line, as well as being an expert magician.

And each was completely and utterly devoted to his hobby as a magician.

The conjuring novice has the world of magic at his feet as soon as he joins a magicians' club.

CHAPTER SIX

MEET THE MAGIC CIRCLE

AT the foot of a flight of stone stairs, deep beneath the great Hearts of Oak building in Euston Road, London, you will find a pair of heavy mahogany doors, thick, solid—and closed.

On the right-hand door is a notice: THE MAGIC CIRCLE— MEMBERS ONLY. If you are not a member, only special permission from the council of the Magic Circle can get you through those doors. Such permission is given only after the council are convinced that the visitor is a fit and proper person to enter here. Famous magicians from other countries, notable figures of the theatre, journalists whose names are known to the whole world, radio and television personalities—all must be approved before these doors are open to them.

It would be incorrect to compare the secrets of the Magic Circle with the secrets of, say, Freemasonry or any other secret society. The Circle has no ritual. Its door is guarded by no armed officer of the society. Its procedure is governed neither by tradition nor by dogma. Its secrets are practical rather than symbolical. But those doors are closed against all except members of the society and those who are approved by its officers.

There is a good reason, of course. The secrets of magic must be guarded jealously, or else there would be no magic—only highly skilled juggling of some variety or other. And the talk inside the Magic Circle clubroom is of little else but magic and its secrets.

Come inside. Hear the talk. See what goes on. And unless you already have some smattering of the magician's art, you will go away marvelling, but little wiser than when you entered.

The doors open easily enough to us, who know their secret. We pass through, you and I, and find ourselves in a dimly lit passage extending right and left. To our right is a darkened doorway, where a tiny hidden spotlight plays on a piece of delicate paper sculpture, showing a rabbit emerging from a hat, high on the wall over the door. This is the way to the club theatre. It's a little too early to find any activity there yet, so let's turn to the left.

Here's a table, bearing the members' signature book. If you're interested in casting your eye over the names entered there you'll find some signatures that are pretty famous in the world of magic. There's Robert Harbin (you've seen him often on TV, haven't you?); Tommy Cooper (so he *is* a magician, after all!); Jay Palmer, of New York, playing the Savoy cabaret this week and the Palladium next week; Voltaire, the electrical wizard; Joe Stuthard, the Canadian card manipulator; the Great Levante, touring England with his magical revue; Billy O'Connor and Chris Charlton, two veteran magicians who form a valued link with the Golden Age of Magic; Dai Vernon, of New York—a visitor, like yourself, this Prince of Prestidigitation.

There they all are, with dozens more. For the conjurer, these are names to conjure with.

Leave the book—better sign first, though—and come into the clubroom. It's a long, low-pitched room, with a remarkable system of lighting. From the ceiling hang witches' hats, and the lamps inside them give what some members like to call a "dim, religious light." Others refer to it, less devoutly, as "too damn dim."

At the far end is a refreshment bar, and along the right-hand wall of the long room are several doors. We'll look inside them in a moment.

Here in the foreground is an enormous table. Just now the seats round it are packed with members coping with cups of tea, sandwiches, packs of cards and magazines, all at the same time. I suppose you could call this the reading room, but, as you see, there's precious little reading going on now, apart from a couple of pro's reading next week's calls in *The Stage*, and two young members arguing about this week's *Abracadabra*.

There's a lot of talk, though, and if we can edge another two chairs in we'll sit in on one of these discussions.

On one side of us there's a group debating the advantages of one particular sleight over another. This young man here, with the shock of fair hair and the wry smile, is Alex Elmsley, former President of Cambridge University's Pentacle Club, and today regarded as one of tomorrow's masters of sleight of hand. Still in his early twenties, Elmsley is already years ahead of his contemporaries in sheer digital skill. See him perform the Riffle Pass with a pack of cards. . . . You *didn't* see him perform it? That's fair enough. You weren't meant to. But he *did* perform it. That's the measure of Elmsley's skill, which is the skill that hides skill. A professional magician, this Mr. Elmsley? Not at all. A member of one of the more abstruse professions; magic is his hobby, not his livelihood.

Arguing with him (as he argues readily with everyone) is bespectacled, balding Bobby Bernard, another of the younger members of the Circle. As he argues, Bernard absent-mindedly performs a never-ending Coin Roll with a half-crown. Some day he'll lose this habit. But he'll never lose the skill needed to do it. Watch. The half-crown rolls, almost of its own volition, along the back of his knuckles from finger to finger, dropping into his palm, popping up again, rolling round again, up again . . . It looks so easy, doesn't it? Try it when you get home. No, not here, please. It's too crowded to find your lost coin on the floor.

What's going on at the other side of us?

This character with the bushy white hair and imperial beard is Eric Mason—The Great Masoni, in the theatrical world. Masoni looks more like the popular conception of a wizard than anyone you're likely to see here tonight. With him is Harry Latour, his former stage manager, now in business with a famous photographic agency. They're planning a new illusion for Masoni's next show.

"It'll mean hiring a girl at least six inches shorter than the cabinet," muses Masoni.

"Not at all," corrects Latour. "Remember? We were going to use a rubber panel in the cabinet. . . ."

Here! Come away! This isn't for visitors!

Before we go, take another look at Harry Latour. Did you ever see that tall, slim figure, those hawk-like features, before? Ever see the original illustrations to the Sherlock Holmes stories in the old *Strand Magazine*? Isn't there an uncanny resemblance here to Paget's wash drawings of Holmes? The odd thing is that Latour's real name is Paget, too. . . .

Here's a distinguished-looking gentleman at the bar, who speaks with a Colonial accent. He's come a long way to the clubroom has Dr. Rolland Frazer, of Sydney, Australia. With him is Bobby Voltaire, whose stage act with electricity is one of the postwar marvels of the variety theatre throughout the world.

Says Dr. Frazer: "Well now, I'm a dentist, so I was able to make the fakes from dental acrylic plastic. And we found that a cigarette would burn for fifteen minutes untended, so we encased it in lead, and . . ."

Voltaire interrupts. "But what about the ammonia?"

"Ah!" says Dr. Frazer, "you're still thinking along the lines of ammonia and acid. You're on the wrong track."

A light illumines Voltaire's face.

"H'm! Could be!" he says. "But who'd have thought that a cigarette . . ."

No use. They've seen us.

The conversation is rapidly switched to the weather. They're both charmed to meet us, but really . . . What you almost heard was one of the really closely guarded secrets of magic. Not more than a dozen people *in the world*, probably, know the inside of that secret.

A big illusion? No. Just a little bit of "business" that takes perhaps half a minute to perform. Here! You mustn't ask any more about that!

Phew!

Look, come in here, out of harm's way.

This is the reference library, as you may guess from the ranks of bookshelves that line the wall, and the piles of books awaiting still more bookcases. Stacked ceiling high here is the biggest collection of books on magic that you'll find in any magical society in the world. Mind you, there are bigger collections existing, but no magicians' club has one to equal this lot. The Harry Price Collection, for example, which is now housed in London University, numbers thousands upon thousands of books—all on magic and allied subjects. In New York's great Public Library are thousands more, legacies from such notable wizards as Harry Houdini and Chung Ling Soo.

Compared with such mammoth collections the Circle's reference library is a modest one. But, as you see, it's still a formidable collection, numbering hundreds of books, many of them exceedingly rare.

The librarian here is Herbert Pratt, by day a London businessman, by night one of Britain's foremost and most erudite bibliophiles. It's not a bit of use asking Bert Pratt to show you a trick—he'd just change the subject. But mention books to him, and he'll talk both your ears off.

Who's this sleek-haired, fresh-faced man with Pratt? This is Chris Charlton, who, believe it or not, was a prominent vaudeville magician touring the world with his own company as long ago as 1910.

And still, despite the dearth of real variety shows, and the over-plenitude of sickly crooners, transatlantic comedians, nude shows and masquerade revues, you'll see Chris Charlton on the bill somewhere or other where an adult (figuratively speaking) audience appreciates outstanding talent rather than artificially built-up "character."

Chris has almost a proprietorial interest in the Circle's reference library, for much of it is based on his own big collection, purchased from him by the Circle a few years ago.

Between ourselves, he leads Bert Pratt the very dickens of a life, seeing to it that his old collection is properly indexed, catalogued and shelved.

Hear them argue now, about some long-defunct magical periodical, some magazine forgotten by everyone except the ardent bookworms.

It's the magazines that chronicle the history of magic, not books such as the one you're reading now. The magazine editor, working to a weekly or a monthly deadline, must work fast, and he must be topical. And so you'll find, recorded in these ancient periodicals, every new sleight, every forgotten fad, all the current tricks and thousands of old ones. You'll find inscribed there every magical scandal of the century, and every legend of long ago. All the madcap magical theories of the ages are debated in their pages, alongside all the sound practicalities that survive to this day.

This reference library of the Magic Circle's contains thousands of such magazines, some bound and indexed, some still wrapped in the yellowing parcels in which they've been stored for half a century and more. Some day—although there's years of work in the job—Bert Pratt, with the persistent heckling and unfailing advice of Chris Charlton, will have them all in smart leather bindings, lined up behind the glass of his growing battery of bookcases.

But it's not all magazines, this repository of the sorceries of an age. Here are reference books too rare to lend out to members, books of which perhaps only two or three copies survive today. Are they valued? They are indeed, and by nobody more than the members who consult them, for there's always some earnest seeker in here, searching, as all magicians must, for the ultimate secrets of their art.

Here you'll find the early editions—three centuries old—of that rarest of magical rarities, *Hocus Pocus Junior*. Here you'll find works on witchcraft dating from the days when people believed in witchcraft. Here you'll find manuscripts circulated for the very, very few, private editions closely guarded by the tiny band of enthusiasts who own them. And side by side with such rarities you'll find the practical modern works, ranging from the paper-bound typescript manuscript on thimble manipulation to the handsome set of six massive volumes of the *Tarbell Course of Magic*.

We could spend a week in here and still leave without having looked into more than a fraction of the books that line this small room. Time's getting on, and there's still more to see, so let's leave Herbert Pratt and Chris Charlton to their never-ending friendly arguments.

This next room? Just the committee room. Nothing in there except members of the council, and I don't suppose you'd want to see *them*. Mind you, if they weren't using this room, we might have popped in and rummaged round some of the interesting equipment of the Occult Committee. Never know what we might find among it, either. They do say, those who've peeped into the boxes and cupboards, that you'll find anything from a ghost to a Swami Gimmick in there. You'd like to know what a Swami Gimmick is? H'm.

Now here, next door, is a place you'll enjoy seeing. It's the Magic Circle's museum. When you leave, you can tell your friends you've seen something unique—actually, not metaphorically, unique. That means there isn't another one like it in the world.

This is Arthur Ivey's domain. Without him, there'd be no museum as we know it today. Arthur Ivey is this pleasant, mild gentleman sitting at his desk just inside the door, one of the most knowledgeable fellows in the world as regards magic and magicians of the past, and chairman of council of the Magic Circle, as well as curator of the museum.

No, don't just browse round at random. That way, you'll never see the things you ought to see, and you'll never get out of here tonight. For this is a fascinating, bewildering wizard's den, this mixture of museum and toyshop, of filing cabinets and showcases. Here is contained the solid, tangible stuff from which has been woven the magic of a century and more.

Here is the actual costume worn by Professor Norris, that remarkable wizard of a hundred years ago; here are the veritable pieces of apparatus he used in his show.

Here is the fishing-rod with which poor ill-starred Chung Ling Soo used to catch living goldfish from the air; here is one of the plates on which he used to catch the bullets fired at him in his "Defying the Bullets" illusion—the bullets which at last killed him on that music-hall stage at Wood Green in 1918.

Here's the table-cloth used by Carl Hertz in his "Devil of a Hat" programme. Look this over carefully and you'll see where many of the incredible objects were stowed before they came out of that one top hat. But look as carefully as you like, and you'll never learn how they found their way into the hat.

Here are Japanese Magic Mirrors—a whole shelf of them. Made of a secret bronze alloy, highly polished on the face and boldly figured in deep relief on the back, they have a curious property. Reflect the light from the polished face on to a dark surface and you'll see, clearly reproduced there, the design that's carved on the *back* of the mirror, dancing in a flickering pattern of light and shade where there ought to be a clear disc of reflected light.

Why? Well, now, people have written books to explain this phenomenon, and it took many hundreds of words to do so. Some other time we'll talk about it. . . .

You've seen the Cups and Balls trick, haven't you? Here are dozens of ancient cups, made of every imaginable metal, wood and papier mâché, that have figured in the trick throughout the world and through the centuries. Here are polished wooden Oriental cups for the same trick, but these, instead of being of the customary goblet shape, are hollow hemispheres with a knob on top, using woollen balls wrapped in fine silk net. But it's the same trick—the trick that fathered the racecourse sharper's swindle with the walnut shells and the pea—and if you look over your shoulder you'll see the picture of a magician performing this very trick four hundred years ago, for the picture was painted as long ago as that.

Trick boxes and cabinets by the score are here. They'll do pretty well everything a magician could wish for, from making an emperor's ring disappear to producing a steaming cup of hot coffee for the blonde in the front row of the stalls.

You'd like to see playing cards? So you shall. Drawer upon drawer of them. Case upon case of them. Frame upon frame of them. Album after album of them. You may have gathered by now that playing cards are especially favoured by the conjurer. Here are square cards, round cards midget cards, giant cards, cards from ancient India, made of ivory, and cards from modern New York, made from plastic, cards of whalebone used by the Eskimos, cards made from slips of bamboo and hailing from China. These? These are tarots. Fortune-telling cards with an incredibly ancient history. Their designs range from the enchanting to the horrific. Their secrets are known to few today.

Now if you really want to see playing cards, we'd better make another appointment with Arthur Ivey, and come and spend a full day over the job.

If you're a privileged visitor, Mr. Ivey may allow you to sit in the handsome plush chair over there. That chair came from the Egyptian Hall, long fallen to the demolition men, where Maskelyne and Cooke made the first real home of magic in London. When the Duke of Edinburgh visited us not long ago, and spent an evening in our theatre and clubroom, he sat in the Egyptian Hall chair. Yes, we value that old chair. We don't think there's another like it in the world.

The posters you see displayed round the clubroom walls are also part of the museum collection. They were set out so that they might be enjoyed by the members, instead of being stowed away in their cabinets. Mounted on silk, their surfaces are specially protected by an invisible film, for they are irreplaceable, these ancient playbills and posters that tell the story of magic now as they told it on the street walls and hoardings so many years ago.

While we've been talking and looking round, the clubroom's filled up. We may just have time to slip into the lending library before the climax of our evening here. Along the corridor and in that next doorway, please.

A counter, with half a dozen bustling assistants behind it. More bookshelves, and books, books, books. In this lending library are well over two thousand volumes on the magic arts. *Two thousand!* It's hard to believe, isn't it, that there could be so many? Here they are, though, and here's the catalogue to prove it. Even so, the Magic Circle lending library only holds a fraction of the books that have been written on the subject.

No time to talk to him now, because there's some activity outside in the clubroom, but over there at the end of the counter, apparently guarding the Occult Section, is librarian Colin Donister. If ever there was a man with an encyclopædic memory, it's Donister. If you'd like to prove it, try keeping a library book a month too long. . . .

And now let's investigate this stir that's going on outside the library.

Down at the end of the long clubroom someone is heartily clanging away at a gong. A stentorian voice roars: "GENTLEMEN! WILL YOU PLEASE TAKE YOUR SEATS IN THE THEATRE!"

And brushing aside the crowds in his way, like a battleship sailing through a flock of ducks, comes the ponderous Sidney Emons, officially styled "Monday Night Host," but in effect a jack of all trades (and master of most) of the Magic Circle club.

If there's anything that will halt this stately march through the room it's a visitor, and—you're the visitor tonight. There's a twinkling, urbane charm about this Sid Emons, a massive hospitality in keeping with the Churchill-size cigar he wields. A real pleasure gleams from behind his spectacles at the prospect of meeting . . . you.

And it's authentic. See him in his restaurant in Pimlico, and you'll get the same welcome. Meet him in the street or on a bus, and the pleasure of the meeting fairly beams from that round face.

Now you're the Magic Circle's guest, and the pleasure of the meeting is doubled for Sidney. A handshake from a hand that could fell an ox. A smile that makes the clubroom lighting look even dimmer than it is. A guiding hand on the elbow in the direction of the theatre. He even calls you "Sir" as he tells you how charmed he is to have the privilege of your company tonight.

While this glowing greeting has been delivered, you've been somehow edged into the theatre at the end of the passage. There's a front-row seat for you, and a parting smile from the portly Emons as he turns to take his seat behind the table on the little stage.

The crowd, now seated, continue their chatter and their endless debates. Mr. Emons smiles in a fatherly manner, and opens his mouth to speak. No sound is heard from him, for the audience are still engrossed in their talk. He opens his mouth again.

This time, the passers-by in the street above could hear him.

"LET'S HAVE A LITTLE HUSH THERE AT THE BACK, PLEASE!" he bellows effortlessly.

There is complete and utter silence.

Now, cooing in a dove-like voice, Mr. Emons gets on with the business of the evening. But first of all, to introduce the guest of the evening.

That's *you.*

Yes . . . get up and bow. See how glad they are to have you with them.

". . . We're delighted to have you with us, sir, and we hope you'll come again!" says Mr. Emons. And if you don't want to come again, after that spontaneous welcome, you're not the man I thought you were.

Now what's on tonight?

First, some new members, to take the obligation of secrecy. And here is Secretary Peter Newcombe, whom you've seen in the Circle's TV shows, to administer the obligation.

You'll hear these new members solemnly undertake never to disclose the secrets of magic to any but magicians. It's a necessary obligation, because so many novice wizards *will* explain just how they do their tricks, when their friends ask them. Then they find that their friends turn away with a superior smirk, saying something like: "But of course! I knew it was done like that. How easy it is, this magic business!"

But when they perform the same tricks *and refuse to tell*, they get a very different reception. Then, it's magic. For the magic of today is clever, wily stuff that challenges detection, until . . . some beginner tells all. Then . . . "But of course! I knew it was done like that!"

As the new members file off the stage, the chairman shuffles a batch of slips of paper. Tonight is a Forum Night, when questions put by members of the audience are answered by the rest of the audience.

First question: "Has anyone a good formula for fireproofing—*really* fireproofing—a pound note?"

And why in the world, you may be thinking, should anyone want to fireproof his money?

My good sir, this is a sensible question, compared with many that magicians ask. Someone once said: "You don't have to be crazy to be a magician . . . but it helps."

The things a magician wants to know are things that nobody else would seek an answer to. And he *needs* to know the answer, for the world of magic is a cockeyed world where people burn money that won't burn, where they struggle for years to find a way to make a piece of thread invisible, where they lose sleep o' nights memorising card set-ups, where they go off their food planning new and devastating manœuvres to obfuscate the patient public.

There now! We've missed the answer to that question. Now we'll never know how to make our folding money fireproof.

Next question: "Isn't it time that television producers paid more attention to camera angles when shooting a magic show?"

Lots of opinions on this, culminating in an authoritative statement from one member, who also happens to be a prominent television producer.

Next question: "Is it fair for a mentalist to make people believe he has some supernormal power?"

Wow! This sets the mentalists at it hammer and tongs. *Who* makes them believe? . . . *Who* makes claims? . . . Who doesn't? . . . Who cares?

Next question: "If I can't get people to pay me a fee for my show, why shouldn't I perform free of charge?"

A HOWL of protest!

"Well, then, is thirty bob too much to ask for an hour's show?"

Dismay! Take this young man aside, someone, and tell him the facts of life! Conjurers must live! (A voice: "Why?" Answer: "Chuck *him* out, too!")

Mr. Emons smiles broadly, and soothes the angry (or hilarious, as the case may be) participants.

"It's generally agreed," he coos, "that if nobody will pay you a fee, it sounds as though your performance isn't worth a fee. And it's also agreed that thirty bob is hardly enough for an hour's show. SIDDOWN!"

Well—it could have been a spoof question. We do get them sometimes, and unless we're very much mistaken, here's one coming up now. . . .

A dignified member rises to ask: "Can anyone tell me whether the Hoffelrimmer Pass is correctly attributed to Dudley Hulme Sinclair?"

A long pause.

Another member rises to ask if this is the same Dudley Hulme Sinclair who worked in a circus and owned a performing bicycle?

A longer pause, slightly thoughtful, this time.

Then a whisper from a much-travelled member at the back of the hall: "I always thought the Hoffelrimmer Pass was a mountain road in Switzerland. . . ."

But wait a moment. Someone's taken the bait at last, and is enlarging on the (entirely imaginary) Hoffelrimmer Pass. Another bethinks himself that he knew a man named Dudley Hulme Sinclair who performed in the streets and sold pills. Yet another thinks that Mr. D. H. Sinclair was a stage violinist doing a tramp act. And soon the opinions and reminiscences of this purely fictitious Dudley Hulme Sinclair are flying thick and fast.

The joke becomes involved, and Mr. Emons, doubled up with laughter, collapses the whole complex fiction. Now hear the laughter! Ah well! It's good for the wits, this occasional sifting of the bogus question from the authentic.

They still talk about the Great Square Balloon Controversy down at the Magic Circle. . . .

Now let's be serious again.

Next question: "Which is the correct version of the Han Ping Chien coin trick?"

Here the sleight of hand experts and the coin men have their moment, and the inquirer leaves the meeting thoroughly briefed and completely satisfied about the execution of this piece of advanced coin magic.

Next question: "The Thumb Tie—is it better to use string, paper-covered cord, or electric flex?"

Now comes a demonstration of each method from members who feature this baffling mystery.

And so they go on, the questions—practical, theoretical, academic, ethical. Even if their significance passes you by, at least you will have realised by now that there is far more to this conjuring business than the mere performance of tricks.

If you'd come last week, you'd have seen something entirely different in this little theatre—Victor Earle's Discoveries. The name "Victor Earle" cloaks the identity of one of London's leading furriers. His "Discoveries" comprise younger members of the Circle, who are thus led to perform their magic in front of their more experienced fellow members. And surprisingly good they are, too.

If you'd chosen next week to visit us, you might have heard a lecture on some technical aspect of magic, or taken part in a competition or a quiz. But this week you've sat in at one of our forums. We hope you liked it—and we hope you'll come again.

The crowd filters out, back into the clubroom. A small body of enthusiasts have been sitting there all the time, round a table where trick tops trick as each participant sets out to baffle the rest.

This is where you'll see the real, the incredible magic.

Watch this one, as shown by young David Berglas.

He holds up a fan of cards, faces towards you, and invites you to think of one of them. Not to take one or touch one, but to *think* of one. You do so. Now he looks at the faces of the cards for the first time, snaps out a card which he holds with its back towards you, at his finger-tips, as he invites you to name the card you thought of. You name it. He turns the single card he holds. It's your card.

Again and again he does it. Even the hardened veterans shake their heads in wonder.

Yes, most of them know how he does it, but for the life of them they can't duplicate the feat every time, as Berglas does.

It was this same Berglas who drove a big left-hand drive American car round some of London's busiest streets one morning last spring—*while heavily blindfolded.* He did this after having his eyes heavily taped and wrapped in surgical bandages by a Harley Street surgeon, just to oblige a newspaper reporter who wanted to see something unusual at the Magic Circle's Golden Jubilee celebrations. What's more, to convince the Pressman, he made him ride in the back of the car.

Berglas is a professional entertainer now. In between bookings he'll slip away to Switzerland, where they know him not as a conjurer but as one of the champions of the Cresta Run. For two pins, I imagine, he'd take his sled down the Cresta Run with a blindfold on. . . .

Here's a quiet-spoken burly chap dealing cards. Nothing unusual in that, you may say, after watching him run swiftly through the pack. There wouldn't be, either . . . if he wasn't dealing them off the bottom of the pack, instead of the top. You have to watch very patiently and closely to see Fred Robinson (a railwayman when he's not doing magic) slip that card from the bottom each time.

Now he deals again. No, no, no. He's not dealing from the bottom now. He's dealing seconds—the card *next* the top one each time.

You wouldn't care to play cards with him? I doubt whether you'd ever persuade him to play at all. Few magicians, nimble as their fingers are with the cards, actually *play*. The cards hold another enchantment for them.

This slender, thoughtful fellow watching so closely is another card man, as many professional card-sharpers know to their cost. He, too, is a railwayman of a sort—a railway detective, who travels on the race trains. If he cared to join in at the Three Card Trick, instead of quietly seeing the tricksters off the train, he could make pretty nice winnings at it. Not only the card-sharpers but the pickpockets on the railways, too, have a wholesome fear of this magician who looks nothing like a magician and still less like a detective—if you don't mind, we won't mention his name. And his expert knowledge of card-sharping and pocket-picking, helped by his long association with magic, is now being passed on to other police forces throughout the country, to whom he delivers official lectures from time to time.

Slowly, while we've been watching, the big clubroom has been emptying. The clock with the Signs of the Zodiac instead of figures on its face tells us, too, that it's time to be going. Goodness! Four hours we've spent here, and only met a tiny proportion of the members, only seen a dozen or so feats of their magic.

Now we must go. If we want to see more, the only thing to do is to come back again some time.

But why come as a visitor? Why not join us yourself?

CHAPTER SEVEN

THE INTERNATIONAL BROTHERHOOD
OF MAGICIANS

YOUNG Len Vintus, a Canadian amateur magician, was a man with a wide circle of friends who corresponded with each other regularly. Over the border in the U.S.A. two of his correspondents were Gene Gordon and Don Rogers. It was in 1923 that these three decided to organise their correspondence society into something a little more binding, a little more lasting, than mere exchanges of letters.

Taking as their symbol the figure of Mercury, messenger of the gods of ancient Olympus—and a magician, too!—they welded their pen-friendships into what soon became known by its present-day title of the International Brotherhood of Magicians.

The background of their badge was the globe of the world, and it was nothing less than the world that they set out to conquer. Theirs was a peaceful conquest, but a positive one.

Today, the International Brotherhood of Magicians is the world's largest organisation of magicians, with more than six thousand members belonging to 142 "Rings" in almost every country of the world.

Those three founder members still wield the wand, but Member No. 4, William W. Durbin, of Kenton, Ohio, U.S.A., passed away in 1937. At the time of his death, Bill Durbin occupied the office of Registrar of the United States under President Franklin D. Roosevelt. His heavy governmental duties, though, never prevented this keen amateur magician from devoting the whole of his leisure time to the society in its young days. As its first President, it was he who organised the world's first magical convention in his private theatre, "The Egyptian Hall," at Kenton, a city which became, and remains to this day, the headquarters of the I.B.M. Since the days of Bill Durbin (with the exception of the war years) the society has held an annual convention in some selected city of the United States.

The I.B.M., though composed mainly of amateur magicians, is by no means amateurish in its business set-up. The affairs of the society are administered by a board of trustees, who meet frequently and work in close co-operation with the International Vice-Presidents appointed in each country possessing a Ring.

There are certain permanent officials, among whom some of the most prominent are the secretary, Dr. A. L. Baldwin; the treasurer-executive secretary, Mrs. Hazel Krock; and the editor of *The Linking Ring*, the society's monthly magazine, Alvin R. Plough. The present (1955) International President of the I.B.M. is C. James McLemore, who, as a former Ring Co-ordinator, was responsible for the formation of a record number of Rings.

What of Britain's contribution to this highly successful and popular International Brotherhood of Magicians?

The British Ring was formed in 1928, and was the twenty-fifth to be established. For sixteen years it had as its President its founder, that brilliantly entertaining professional magician and theatrical journalist, Oswald Rae. Ossy still flourishes, and the years pass him by lightly. Occupying the President's office today is Geoffrey Robinson, widely known to British television audiences for his long series of broadcasts in "Whirligig."

Other Presidents of the British Ring have been Herbert J. Collings (who is now President of the Magic Circle in its Golden Jubilee year), His Honour Ernest C. Wethered, Bill Stickland (British Ring secretary since 1933), John Ramsay, Harry Kaye, John Gambling and Oscar Paulson.

That list of British Ring Presidents is a lively reminder of the happy democracy of magic. There you have, among others, a chartered accountant, a society entertainer, a judge, a Scottish grocer, a businessman, a retired civil servant and a communications engineering executive.

Of the original founder members of the British Ring, four—Oswald Rae, Walter Kemp, Professor Bofeys and Joe Rendell—are all still happily with us as honorary life members. Of two others, the Ring lost Professor Ducarell through death, and Nelson Denys gave up conjuring to enter the Church.

The Ring's first secretary, who served in that office until 1933, was Dleisfen, a magician of considerable note at that time. His successor, and the present secretary, is the burly but energetic Bill Stickland. It seems odd to mention Bill by himself, for, it seems, the term is always "Bill Stickland and Poppy." He and his wife, who is his partner in magic as well as matrimony, are invariably named together, and are the guiding spirits behind the mammoth conventions held by the British Ring each year. During the war, as ENSA artistes, they were the first magicians to cross the Rhine, and were giving their show in Hamburg two days after that city fell to the Allies.

Some idea of the ramifications of the British Ring can be had by a glance at the comprehensive list of officers serving the society at the time of writing. They include: Jeffery Atkins, a prominent Southampton businessman, who is honorary treasurer; Voltaire, editor of the Ring's excellent magazine, *The Budget*; Freddy Carter, honorary auditor; Donald Crombie, honorary solicitor; Eddie Dexter, welfare officer; Robert Johnson, publicity officer; and Bill West, librarian.

As you may expect, these are skilled magicians. But they are also highly efficient officers of the society. To take one example: Eddie Dexter, of Southport, holds down what would be for many people a full-time job as welfare officer. If a member of the society is sick, Eddie has him supplied with those little extras that so often mean rapid convalescence. He also makes sure that his fellow members hear about the invalid, who is likely to receive showers of gifts, books, magazines, fruit, cigarettes, letters, visits—the LOT!

A well-known magician and comedian, Arthur Dowler, was gravely ill at his home at Brighton some few years ago. As soon as the news got around, the British Ring, inspired by Eddie Dexter, got to work. Arthur's letter-box was seldom empty after that. And when convention time came round, member after member wrote and sent him souvenirs of the big occasion. More than that—scores of members got together and sent him one huge "get well" letter, signed by all of them.

Poor Arthur died—there was little hope of his recovery at any time, and the Ring knew it—but one of his last, and happiest memories, was the loving-kindness of his fellow members of the International Brotherhood of Magicians.

Brotherhood—that's the word the members of the I.B.M. like to live up to.

"We feel," says secretary Bill Stickland, "that by bringing together magicians of all races and creeds, bound by a common love of magic, we are contributing in some small measure to the peace of the world and a better understanding among nations." A modest claim, but one which other organisations might well try to adopt.

They have a benevolent fund, too, have these charitable conjurers, but, beyond mentioning, almost in passing, that it is under the control of a board of trustees (Donald Crombie, Arthur Culpin, Eddie Dexter, Edward Love and Bill Stickland), they are modestly reticent about it. Which is, I suppose, as it should be. But I can disclose that their benevolent fund has done magnificent work for those members who are sick or in distressed circumstances. Their names are known to the trustees and a few officials, but beyond that the benevolent fund's administrators keep such details to themselves. Which is, again, as it should be.

The names of the British Ring committee, if assembled on a playbill, would provide a programme of rare talent. There is founder Oswald Rae, whom many ex-Servicemen will recall for his delightfully witty shows while touring with ENSA during the war. I remember meeting him in Alexandria's tiny Globe Theatre in 1944, in between whirlwind tours (in more senses than one) of the Western Desert and other cheerless spots in the Middle East. Not for him the delights of a peaceful life in Alexandria; he was all agog for his next tour of the troops in the desert.

Bobby Voltaire is another member of the committee. Now here is a magician with the most terrific sense of showmanship you'll see in many a long year. Voltaire is a professional vaudeville magician, and where less aspiring conjurers use playing cards, silk handkerchiefs, billiard balls or thimbles, Voltaire uses POWER, in the shape of blinding, high-tension electricity. He will pluck a bulb from the footlights, hold it at arm's length, tense every muscle—*and light the bulb*. No wires, no flex—just magic!

And, in case you doubt the evidence of your eyes, he will hand the bulb to *you*, as you sit in the stalls. While you hold it (and furtively examine it for secret gimmicks!) Voltaire will *still* light the bulb, from his position on the stage yards away. And if that's not magic, then tell me what it is.

Bobby will send you away from the theatre dazzled, not only with his lighting of an unconnected lighthouse lamp, but with his sheer impressive skill and personality. If you meet him offstage, he is quite likely to show you a little crystal star; some sort of decoration that was presented to him during a European tour, he will tell you. There it sits, in his lapel. He will take it out, and you, of course, will want to handle it and admire it. He will replace it, show you back and front of the coat lapel—and will light the little star by breathing on it.

Although his mind seems to run constantly on the complexities of his particular kind of magic, Voltaire and his charming wife, Gwen, stage a particularly beautiful little show for children when the occasion arises. Martha, "the world's only electronic dog," may well take part in it. Martha is a tiny, tiny Yorkshire terrier who lives in a glass kennel. If you don't see Martha on the stage, you'll find her, all twelve ounces of her, guarding the Voltaires' dressing room against all comers.

Voltaire has an entertaining kind of magic that goes several steps farther, both in entertainment and in magic, than did that of the late spectacular Dr. Walford Bodie.

Peter Warlock is the third member of the British Ring committee. The name conceals the identity of an official of the Midland Bank, who lives at Wallington, in Surrey, and who enjoys a world-wide reputation as a performer and magical inventor.

Warlock's magic is of the mental kind usually, and he dispenses with the normal apparatus of the conjurer. He will read your mind infallibly, under the right conditions. He will do more than that: he will predict accurately what you are *going* to think in five minutes' time. His newspaper headline predictions, often made weeks ahead, have set magicians, as well as the public, guessing everywhere.

Warlock edits a magazine for the advanced magician—*The Pentagram*. Read it carefully, and unless you are well beyond the stage of the parlour trickster it will mean nothing to you. But to the expert, Warlock's *Pentagram* has brought some masterly secrets and information.

In addition to his other claims to fame, Peter Warlock is the father of slim, attractive Elizabeth Warlock, who has more than once walked away with the major trophy for skill at international contests of magic . . . leaving her father as runner-up on at least one occasion. They do say, those magical critics who sit in the back rows, that Elizabeth may some day be a better witch than her father is a Warlock. But they never let Peter know it—or Elizabeth.

Down at Cheam, in Surrey, there's a builder's merchant by the name of Francis Haxton. Big, broad, smiling Francis is another member of the Ring committee. See him at the card table, with nothing more than a pack of cards and those incredibly deft fingers, and you will see pure wizardry. Haxton is by no means the sort of chap you would picture as a card trickster. No smooth, slick line of patter goes with his miracles. No hint of flashiness mars his impeccable appearance. No fast move raises your suspicions—and your hopes that you have caught him out. Slowly, softly, in a modest, grave voice, Haxton will tell you that he proposes that you shall handle the cards *yourself*. You shuffle them, you cut them, you deal them completely at random into two piles, face down. You turn over the cards . . . and you find that somehow you have dealt all the red cards into one pile and all the black cards into the other. "Out of this world!" I've heard magicians murmur when seeing this feat.

Francis Haxton is one of the original "Flying Sorcerers," a tiny collection of conjurers who, by invitation, fly the Atlantic from time to time to baffle the magicians of America.

Another "Flying Sorcerer" is Tom Harris, a Derby businessman, who is also a member of the British Ring committee. And American magicians say of him, too, that his magic is out of this world. True, they sometimes add thoughtfully that it's because they can't understand a word Tom is saying. As a schoolmaster, in cap and gown, Tom Harris treats his audience— whether it's composed of countesses or colliers—as his class. And a tough taskmaster he is, too, dealing out clips on the ear and hearty abuse generously to his luckless but hilarious volunteer assistants. I have heard it suggested that Tom Harris's bill matter should be altered from "The Schoolmaster Magician" to "The Riot Act." You can't analyse Tom Harris's brand of humour—but you're safe in saying, as everyone who's seen him says, that it's first-rate entertainment.

George Blake is another North-country magician whose reputation extends round the world. He, too, is a member of the British Ring committee, where his erudite skill and inventive genius is deeply appreciated. He is a writer on magical subjects, who was for a long time editor of the British Ring magazine *The Budget*, and who must by now have lost count of his innumerable magical creations.

Another committee member who is a well-known magical writer is Edward Love, a perfectionist whose book on Card Fanning is the standard text-book on the subject. He is a scholarly expert on the techniques of magic, and his writings, all too few, are going to be rare treasures of the magician's library in a few years' time.

Academic qualifications count for a lot among knowledgeable magicians. Committee member Jack Potter is an example in point. Jack, who lives at Stockport, is probably one of the most widely read magicians of this or any day. He has an encyclopædic knowledge of the practicalities of conjuring, and for some time now has been editing a feature called "Potter's Bar"¹ in *The Budget*. This sets out to do no less than catalogue every magical effect in all its variations. The bibliography Potter is compiling will be unique when—if ever—it is completed. He aims to list every published trick, so that the student, by consulting "Potter's Bar," may have chapter and verse at his disposal.

Those who entertain children do their magic the hard way, for the dear little teeny-weenies are somewhat uninhibited, and are apt to screech "Seen it before!"—a dreaded cry, which is now being supplanted by "Seen it on telly!" But your skilled children's entertainer does not fear this contretemps. Wilfred Tyler, a committee member who is an insurance official in Sheffield, rarely hears "Seen it before!" from his juvenile audiences, for he is an originator and adaptor of great aptitude, and what he shows the children is invariably his own treatment of a trick. He, too, is a writer of note, and has written text-books on the art of entertaining children, which is one of the most highly specialised branches of the entertainer's art. The very thought of showing to the kids raises goose pimples on many a hardened magician, but not on Tyler. He loves it, and, let it be noted, makes a very nice thing out of it, both artistically and financially.

A solicitor's clerk in the little Herefordshire town of Ledbury was christened Eric Williams. Today, he is a member of the British Ring committee, and is better known as Eric Nitwit Williams. Never, I do assure you, will you see such a solemnly mad *pavane* of prestidigitation as that presented by Eric Williams and His Ma (for Mrs. Williams is his onstage and offstage assistant, and without her placid, long-suffering aid there might be none of the Nitwit's mad miracles). He will show you a monstrous cactus in a flower-pot, will tell you in a dramatic whisper that it blossoms once in every fifty years—"And tonight's the night!" It does blossom, too, after due ritual and incantation by the audience. He will invite your attention to his cataleptic rat, a horrifying thing that scampers all over the stage—and then vanishes.

One loses count of all the Eric Williams characters one has seen. There is his "Madame Frisson, the Lady Magician from Paris," who will shake a roguish hip at you, lowering eyelids fringed with three-inch lashes. There is his eerie schoolgirl magician, worthy of Hermione Gingold at her archest. There is his curious cowboy, who carries his horse's false teeth in his pocket. There is his Eastern wonder-worker with the mat that conceals the most remarkable objects.

He's no fool, this madcap magician, though. I remember hearing him lecture to the Magic Circle some years ago on "Carefree Conjuring." The way he talked, and the way he had things arranged, his show seemed to work itself. One of his ingenious contrivances involved a pack of cards nailed into one solid block. I must not reveal what they were used for—but I can say that they enabled their inventor to perform a trick which overwise might have meant years of practice of sleight of hand.

Eric Williams may stage his show in a West Country village hall one night and in a glossy West End cabaret the next. He is equally at home—and his audience is equally convulsed—in either.

That, then, is a brief introduction to the committee members of the British Ring. What of the members themselves?

The British Ring of the International Brotherhood of Magicians has faithfully followed the example set by its parent society, for, from a small beginning, membership has now grown to more than 900. But, convinced that quality is more important than quantity, the committee some years ago introduced their Interrogation Officers scheme, whereby all candidates for membership are interviewed by specially appointed I.B.M. officers, who have to be satisfied that the applicants are suitable for membership before they are admitted.

Serving as an invaluable and permanent link between the 900 or so members is the Ring's monthly magazine, The Budget, which started as a mimeographed sheet and is now a printed book of many pages, crammed with information and entertainment.

The Budget serves the British Ring exclusively, but available to all I.B.M. members is their international organ, The Linking Ring. This is today the largest magical magazine the world has ever seen, and its quality measures up well to that standard. It averages 170 pages per issue, and since Alvin Plough took over the editorship it has developed into a publication that is highly prized by its readers. If a copy of *The Linking Ring* falls into your hands, you will want to see the next issue and to read it regularly. But unless you have been accepted as a member of the I.B.M., *The Linking Ring* is not for you. It's a members-only publication, and if the I.B.M. could offer no other inducement its *Linking Ring* would ensure a high membership figure.

And does the member of the British Ring ever meet any of his 899 and more fellow-members? It's his own fault if he doesn't, for there are opportunities regularly enough.

The founders of the I.B.M. in America set the vogue and established the pattern for magical conventions, and the British Ring has followed closely in the founders' footsteps. In this country, as in the U.S.A. and other countries overseas, an I.B.M. Convention is held every summer. The first British Ring Convention was held in the garden of Professor Bofeys, at Cheltenham. Today, the mammoth size of these gatherings calls for tremendous organising skill and long-term planning. Each is attended by hundreds of British and foreign magicians. The convention-wise conjurer needs no further elucidation when asked if he is going "to the Convention." He takes it for granted that it's the I.B.M. Convention you mean, and he will be well posted on time, place and all the other details.

Yes, they are important dates in the conjurer's calendar, these conventions. The same goes for the date of the annual British Ring Dinners. One is held in London, and there is often another in the provinces during the winter.

Other functions take place at frequent intervals, including a Christmas party, London shows, a summer picnic, and many special gatherings arranged at long or short notice, as the case may be, to welcome celebrated magical visitors to this country.

When Len Vintus, Gene Gordon and Don Rogers got together and decided to call their correspondence club the International Brotherhood of Magicians in 1923, they can have had no conception of the magnitude of the thing they were starting. Today, they see it, more than six thousand strong, extending round the world and back again.

It is truly International, and it is equally truly—a Brotherhood.

CHAPTER EIGHT

THESE ARE NAMES TO CONJURE WITH

NAMES to conjure with!
Surely, the greatest names in the magic of this century are those of Maskelyne and Devant, although no Maskelyne has performed on the stage of this country for five years and more, and although David Devant last presented his brilliant style of conjuring as long ago as 1914. Poor Devant! When he died, in the Putney Home for Incurables in 1941, he had suffered twenty years of almost complete paralysis.

In his last, failing years, members of the Magic Circle used to visit the hospital regularly to perform for him. Now, to honour his memory, they pay an annual visit there to entertain the patients with their David Devant Memorial Programme.

The long tale of Maskelyne's starts in Cheltenham in the 1860's, when young John Nevil Maskelyne, a local watchmaker, succeeded in unmasking the notorious Davenport Brothers, fraudulent "spiritualist" wonder-workers.

J. N. (he is rarely known by any longer name among the magical fraternity) had been working in his shop when a stranger brought in a delicate piece of mechanism that needed slight repair.

"If you could tell me what this is to be used for, I could perhaps make a better job of it," said J. N.

But the stranger was evasive, and handed over a much larger sum of money than was needed to pay for the work.

"I've no doubt a smart young fellow like you could use the change," he said slyly, adding: "And in return, just forget you ever met me!"

Life in Cheltenham then, as now, moved smoothly and slowly, and so when a few days later the Cheltenham Town Hall Assembly Rooms were booked by the Davenport Brothers for their strange and eerie performance the whole town was agog. But in the meantime young John Nevil Maskelyne had been doing some hard thinking—and some rather secret work at his watchmaker's bench. The Davenports, he had heard, included in their programme demonstrations of table rapping. Ira Davenport, whose picture now placarded the town, was a man with long hair and a silky beard. It was just such a man, speaking with a strong American accent, who had brought the curious bit of apparatus to J. N. for repair.

The strange piece of mechanism was nothing less than the secret device that produced the "spirit" raps on the table in their performance, and J. N. produced an identical machine. It was surely something more than the long arm of coincidence that had thrown Ira Davenport in the way of the young Cheltenham watchmaker, for even in those days J. N. was something of an amateur conjurer. With his friend George Cooke he had given presentable little shows in and around Cheltenham, and had inspired other youngsters with a fancy for the magic arts.

Like the bogus spiritualists today, the Davenports insisted on a darkened room for their performance, and this aroused J. N.'s suspicions—as it has aroused many, many suspicions since that day. Accordingly, he arranged for one of the blinds of the Assembly Rooms to be opened a little at that particular stage of the performance when the Davenports were supposed to be securely tied hand and foot.

All was progressing most impressively, and the bound Davenports seemed to be producing the most convincing phenomena of "spirit" activities.

Suddenly, a shaft of light shone down on them, and they were seen to be free of their bonds and in the middle of producing a particularly astonishing piece of "spirit" phenomena.

At once they leapt back to their chairs and resumed their bonds, but it was too late. Not only John Nevil Maskelyne, but the whole audience, had caught the sharpers in the act of cheating.

Later, J. N. and Cooke reproduced all the "phenomena" that the Davenports had produced, but this time in full view of the audience and without the merciful curtain of darkness.

Encouraged by their success, Maskelyne and Cooke threw up their jobs and took to the road as travelling magicians. In 1867 they were booked to perform at the Crystal Palace, and within six years had become so well known that they could take their growing company to the St. James's Great Hall in Piccadilly. After a month or so there, they moved a few doors down Piccadilly to the small hall at the Egyptian Hall, where Maskelyne's were to have their home—and "England's Home of Mystery"—for nearly thirty years.

It was in 1904 that J. N., against all advice, took over St. George's Hall, in Langham Place, and there Maskelyne's Mysteries stayed until changes of partnership and war broke up the old syndicate of sorcery. Nazi bombs put the finishing touch to things by breaking up the hall itself.

The name of Maskelyne ran like a golden thread through all the years of

"England's Home of Mystery," but the other partner—Cooke—dropped out in favour of David Devant when the St. George's Hall venture started.

Devant had joined the company in 1893, and had rapidly assumed the position of the more popular performer of the two. His polished, suave, witty style was greatly to the liking of the crowds who flocked to the Egyptian Hall and later to Langham Place. His inventive turn of mind brought money to the Maskelyne and Devant coffers, and many new illusions, as well as smaller mysteries, were due to his initiative and hard work.

In 1914, after Devant had retired, J.N.'s son, Nevil Maskelyne, entered the partnership. It only lasted another three years in that form, for in 1917 John Nevil Maskelyne died at the age of 78.

It had been an adventurous life for J. N. Always an aggressive figure, he flung himself with enthusiasm into a controversy. In 1906 he wrote a letter to the *Daily Telegraph* expressing strong views about spiritualism, which led to the famous lawsuit with Archdeacon Colley, Rector of Stockton. A challenge to duplicate certain "spiritualistic phenomena" was promptly flung out by the Archdeacon, and as promptly snapped up by J. N. The Archdeacon said that he had deposited £1,000 with his bankers, to be paid to J. N. if he could do what the mediums had done for the Archdeacon.

The resultant litigation included the unusual spectacle of a special jury in the King's Bench Division, with Mr. Justice Ridley, sitting in the stalls of St. George's Hall to judge for themselves whether J. N.'s presentation on the stage matched what Archdeacon Colley claimed for *his* phenomena.

And there on the stage, John Nevil Maskelyne and his assistant, clad in long black frock-coats and clerical collars, performed their amazing reproduction of a materialisation seance, in which a "spirit" appeared to issue from the left side of one of the performers.

But alas! J. N. lost the case, forfeited £75 damages for libel, and lost £1,000.

He was a spectacular figure in his later days, was "Old Man Maskelyne," as he came to be known. I have often heard Herbert J. Collings, President of the Magic Circle, tell of his odd little ways in the theatre. Herbert Collings performed at St. George's Hall many times, and he will tell you that one of the most spectacular and truly difficult of all the feats performed there—or anywhere else—was the plate-spinning act of J. N. A number of china plates and bowls were kept spinning by a mere occasional touch of the finger from J. N., apparently with no trouble at all and the most perfect ease. So easy was the trick—or so it looked—that J. N. would stand spinning his plates and gazing amiably out at the audience.

"But," says Herbert Collings, with a chuckle, "the artful old boy was counting the house, and woe betide the box office if their receipts didn't tally with what J. N. reckoned they should have taken!"

J. N. used to wear a ring with an enormous diamond while he performed the plate spinning, and the electrician on the spotlight was careful always to ensure that the ring came in for a good share of the limelight. As a result, tiny flashes of light from the diamond scintillated as J. N.'s deft hands moved among the whirling crockery, throwing out beams like a miniature lighthouse.

John Nevil Maskelyne, remember, had been trained as watchmaker, a skilled craftsman in small mechanisms. His greatest triumph, to my mind, was with his automata—artificial figures which would apparently perform many things that only a practised human could do. This was before Karel Capek coined the word "robot," and Maskelyne's automata were known, for simplicity's sake, by the names he bestowed on them. After all, "automata" is a tricky word to get the tongue round, and J.N. knew well that if you want the public to remember and talk about a thing you must give it a name they can remember—and can repeat.

His first robot figure, "Psycho," was made as a result of his collaboration with John Algernon Clarke, a Lincolnshire farmer, in 1873. Clarke had been trying to perfect an idea for a machine which could play cards.

When J. N. brought his brain to the task, the result was Psycho—which not only played cards and won, but also performed lightning calculations and a few conjuring tricks.

You may see Psycho himself today in the London Museum. He is a benign, smallish Hindu figure, seated cross-legged on a small plinth mounted on a clear glass pillar. When Psycho played three members of the audience at whist, J. N. would lay the cards before him on his plinth, in a vertical slide. When Psycho had to play a card, his hand would pass along the frame until it reached the correct card, which he would lift slowly and thoughtfully before laying it on the table for the audience to see.

His mathematical calculations were carried out with the aid of small tablets, each bearing a figure, which were placed in another frame.

There were many rumours afoot that Psycho was hollow, and that his interior concealed a legless dwarf. The same tale had been told, nearly thirty years earlier, of the automata made and exhibited by Robert-Houdin, the famous French magician. It had been told, too, of that miraculous performing figure owned by Baron von Kempelen, of Vienna—the Chess Player. Robert-Houdin himself, in his memoirs, flatly states that von Kempelen's Chess Player was motivated by a Pole named Worousky, who, being tiny in stature, was rendered even smaller by the loss of both legs in battle. It may be, of course, that Robert-Houdin was following that deplorable practice—once common among conjurers—of pretending to expose another's illusion in order to point out that his own could not possibly be performed in the same way.

But if you look closely at Psycho in the London Museum, I think you will agree that it would only house a very tiny dwarf. And it would have been even more difficult for Maskelyne to find a pocket-size legless dwarf who could beat all comers at whist than it would have been for him to have the illusion performed by mechanical means.

The glass pillar, I have always thought, hides the secret of Psycho's operation. Nowadays, there is more than one illusion which depends upon the transparency of glass for its success. One thing is pretty certain: Psycho would not play whist with you or me in his new home at the London Museum. He was more at home on the elaborately fitted stage of Maskelyne's theatre in Piccadilly.

When the audiences at the Egyptian Hall were allowed to examine Psycho's interior—in which they only found a complex mass of machinery—you may guess that Psycho himself was only the concluding end of the illusion. His main "works" were probably at some distance from the stage. And the machinery in his inside probably had nothing whatsoever to do with his working.

Although the simple Hindu, with his glass pillar and his marvellous internal mechanism, may not have known it, he was almost certainly the father of many of the later miracles that Maskelyne exhibited. For it had been necessary, in order to build Psycho with all due secrecy, to have a large workshop built at the Egyptian Hall, and it was there that Psycho was constructed. It was in that same workshop that many other of the large-scale Maskelyne illusions were made.

Psycho had several successors and imitators.

Dr. Pepper, of Pepper's Ghost fame, exhibited a similar automaton, "Cynthia," at Sadler's Wells. But Cynthia, alas, broke down and refused to play chess or anything else.

His more legitimate successors, from the Maskelyne workshops, included "Zoe," a modest little lady who could sketch the profile of a member of the audience, "Fanfair," who played the cornet, and "Labial," who performed upon the euphonium. These two last-named, according to Jasper Maskelyne, writing in *White Magic*, " . . . were scholarly little men with the long locks and dreamy eyes of true musicians. One sat on a chair and the other on a music stool. They were set in the middle of the stage, free from any connection with the sides, roof or—apparently—the floor, and they performed sweetly and accurately any popular piece of music asked for by the audience. Highbrow or low, it was all the same to them. The audience could come up and examine them from every side. No works were apparent, no clockwork ticking or whirring was audible, there were no electric wires or air-pipe connections. There they sat, mysterious, complacent and earnest, and a good deal more human than some modern musicians I have met."

The automata were regarded by J. N. as members of his family, and he not only made all their mechanisms, built their faces, hands and feet, inserted their teeth and eyelashes, but supervised the very cut of their clothes.

"They were as much his children," says grandson Jasper Maskelyne, "as were my father and uncle."

If John Nevil Maskelyne was the brain behind Maskelyne and Devant's, David Devant was the showpiece. A skilled sleight of hand expert, he never fell into the trap so many "finger-flingers" find themselves in. Always, entertainment, rather than blatant skill, was the prime object of his performance.

His was the sleight of hand that was never, never apparent—the skill that hides skill.

Devant was at his best when performing illusions that required the assistance of children from the audience. Never, since Devant's day, have we had such a master of magic for—and with—children.

One veteran performer who often played a Maskelyne and Devant booking never tires of praising Devant's sound knowledge of child psychology. With a chuckle, he will tell you of the first time there was catastrophe on the stage. One small child who mounted the steps to assist the magician showed distressingly fidgety signs as soon as she found herself on the stage. A moment later, there was a howl of dismay from the child, and a growing pool on the floor!

"After that," says my friend, "Devant and the stage staff were prepared. Devant seemed to be able to read a child's mind, and if ever such a doubtful customer appeared on the stage after that first episode, she (it was nearly always she!) was whisked into the wings, where a rather necessary piece of utility crockery had been installed for the occasion."

Devant shone, too, in the famous sketches that were performed at St. George's Hall. One of them, "Will, the Witch and the Watchman," was revived—with the original cumbersome apparatus and scenery—at a recent Magic Circle Festival of Magic at the Scala Theatre in London. The Magic Circle, though, under no delusions as to the difficulty of duplicating the Devant presentation, hired actors to play the chief parts.

But for magicians, the true high-spot of Devant's part of the programme always came when he depended upon his sleight of hand. Devant could turn into an enthralling and amusing playlet that rather featureless trick, the Multiplying Billiard Balls. When it came to the Eggs from the Hat, too, he had the audience rocking with laughter—mainly because the scores and scores of real eggs produced from an empty hat soon became too large a load for the juvenile assistant. There would be eggs all over the place, with Devant blandly and unwittingly producing still more, which were piled in the child's arms.

In July 1912, Devant was bidden to perform at the Royal Command show at the Palace Theatre. For this occasion, his child assistants were his own daughter, Vida, and young nine-year-old Jasper Maskelyne, grandson of J. N. It is recorded, alas, that Jasper showed greater interest in the Royal Box and its occupants than in the magic he was supposed to be assisting. He admits that he kept a sharp eye on the Royal Box through most of the act, at last demanding of Devant, in a piercing whisper: "Where are their crowns?"

Devant was one of the truly great writers on magic, as well as being the master magician of his time. At one time, his writings got him into trouble, for the Magic Circle requested him to resign from that society. It is one of the Magic Circle's aims to prevent the explanation of magical secrets to the public, and when Devant wrote—as many have written before and since—a series of articles explaining simple tricks in a magazine, he fell foul of the society of which he had been a president. Out he went, gracefully and unrelenting, but it was not long before the Circle made up the quarrel. Today, Devant's name is revered as no other magician's is by the Magic Circle.

But the writings of Devant that will live longest are those he did for conjurers. Although many—if not all—of his books were on sale to the public, the anti-exposers seemed to take little offence. C. Arthur Pearson published, in a bright yellow cover, several of his books at two shillings each. If you can buy a copy in good condition today it is worth ten times that sum.

His greatest book was shared with Nevil Maskelyne, son of J. N. Together they wrote *Our Magic*, a text-book on the art and practice of conjuring. In its day, there was difficulty in selling it at something like seven shillings and sixpence. Today a copy costs anything from £2 to £5, according to condition.

Our Magic is, frankly, heavy going through Maskelyne's chapters on the art *in* magic (he insisted on "the art *in*" and not "the art *of*"). But when it has been read three or four times, its contents are priceless. The pity is, though, that far too few present-day readers trouble their sawdust-filled heads with Maskelyne's theories. "Can't plough through all that stuff!" they say scornfully, probably adding: "In any case, I don't agree with all of it."

Devant's share of the book was equally priceless. In it, he describes, move by move, word by word, several of his most famous tricks and illusions. One can almost see and hear him at work, in reading this book. The photographs (the American edition, published by Fleming, has substituted line drawings) bring back that delightful, Edwardian, arty-crafty stage at St. George's Hall, with its potted palms and its lattice-work, its solid appurtenances and its garden sets and chamber sets (which had nothing to do with the problem of child assistants!)

There is Devant, handsome handlebar moustache and sweeping tail coat, going through the mysteries that must, through the years, have become second nature to him. And yet never once did one suspect that he was performing a trick other than for the first time. Always fresh, always smiling, always friendly and amusing—poor Devant. He was to come to a painful and lingering end.

The last time I saw him was in 1925 when he was on holiday at St. Annes-on-Sea, in Lancashire. He was being wheeled round the open-air baths. For two hours I, a magic-struck youth, stalked his wheel chair, until at last I plucked up courage to speak to him. His manservant, wheeling the chair, shook his head silently at me in warning. It was not one of Devant's good days, and he was hardly able to speak. But—I can say that I once met and spoke to Devant. Bless him. There was nobody like him.

Although there was never to be another Devant to enchant us with his mysteries, the name of Maskelyne survived for years after the death of J. N. First of all, Nevil, his son, headed the St. George's Hall company until his death in 1926. From him Jasper Maskelyne, son of Nevil, took over, at the age of twenty-four—no doubt the youngest theatre manager in London.

Writing in *White Magic, the Story of Maskelyne's*, Jasper has this to say about the heavy responsibilities he inherited:

"I had not had enough experience to make me sure of myself in my new rôle; and though later I became managing director, it was with very considerable qualms.

"Presenting magic is one thing; controlling the destinies of a place with such a tradition as that of St. George's Hall is another.

"I combed the world for talent; I sought out artistes and illusions in the most unlikely places. I worked about twenty hours a day, in the workshops making apparatus, on the stage rehearsing, or actually giving or superintending performances.

"I think I did pretty well. . . ."

That is a modest description of Jasper Maskelyne's work. Until he parted company with the controlling body at St. George's Hall he put on first-rate shows there. Then, in 1933, there was disagreement between members of the family controlling St. George's Hall, and Jasper, in his own words, was dismissed.

Had the family been able to retain his services, we might still have a

"Home of Mystery" in London, for Jasper Maskelyne carried on the family tradition for several years before and after the 1939-45 war. Touring the music-halls and cine-variety of this country, Europe and the Dominions, he ably carried on the work that his grandfather had begun in the 1860s. During the war he lent his talents to the Government, and for a time was stationed in the Middle East, where, as a camouflage officer, he had a big share in the Western Desert battles, and in the final campaign that turned Rommel at Alamein.

I remember sitting near him in the lounge of the Cecil Hotel in Alexandria one evening, when a native gully-gully man came in with his bag of tricks. He showed the Cups and Balls and a trick or two with snakes, and after collecting his backsheesh made his way out. In a few seconds he was back, highly indignant. Some *klifty wallad*, he declared, had stolen his chicks and his snakes.

Walking round the lounge glaring accusingly at everyone, he finally turned out his cloth bag to show where the chicks and snakes had been—to find that they were back there once more. And in one corner where the gully-gully man had paused for a moment, sat Major Maskelyne, chuckling quietly to himself. Had the Egyptian youth known, he might have learnt a trick or two to add to his repertoire that evening!

With the war over, Jasper Maskelyne resumed his touring activities, and staged several seasons' shows at London's Westminster Theatre. In his last season there—in 1947—there was one amusing episode about which conjurers are still laughing. In the company was Kuda Bux, that amazing Kashmiri performer—"The Man with the X-Ray Eyes"—who is now in America. Another artiste on the bill was one Donna Delbert, "The Only Lady Fire-Eater in the World."

Donna Delbert put on a good show of conjuring, whip-cracking and fire-eating. Some weeks later, the newspapers carried headlines: "American Deserter Poses as Woman Magician." Donna Delbert was none other than Don Delbert, Pfc., U.S. Armed Forces, who had been absent without leave for many a moon. Delbert took things philosophically when he was arrested by the American redcaps, and the last I saw of him was a burly figure, now wearing a moustache, seated in a jeep between two redcaps and smoking a cigar. The court martial was over, and Pfc. Don Delbert was off to serve his sentence.

But, magicians kept asking one another, what about The Man with the X-Ray Eyes, who had performed on the same bill? What about those X-Ray Eyes? Hadn't *they* spotted Donna Delbert's guilty secret?

But if they hadn't, we mustn't blame Kuda Bux. Delbert's impersonation was convincing indeed. I once met him in his dressing room at a Magic

Circle show, and came out without a suspicion that he was anything but "The Only Lady Fire-Eater in the World." I even had several conversations with him afterwards, when he sought advice about securing concert bookings in London, and bewailed the fact that a young girl had a hard time getting in the agents' good books!

The fact is that not a soul at the Westminster Theatre had any inkling that Delbert was a man. To everyone—until he was caught by the redcaps— he was every inch a lady.

That 1947 season at the Westminster was the last occasion on which many of us saw Jasper Maskelyne's pleasant magic. And pleasant it was. He was in his element with a crowd of children on the stage, and I don't think I have ever seen *any* performer, magical or otherwise, who could handle children as Jasper handled them. He would treat them as equals, sitting down on the floor to discuss, with knitted brow and solemn features, some knotty mystery that puzzled them. And he would send them back to their seats perfectly delighted with that lovely magician they'd just been "helping!"

Jasper Maskelyne had several outstanding tricks and illusions by which I shall always remember him. There was, first and foremost, his marvellous Chinese make-up for some of his items. When Jasper stepped on to the stage in that make-up he *was* a Chinese—an old, venerable, wise Chinese magician.

There was his smooth presentation Swallowing Razor Blades, a trick we've all seen scores of times, but which always seemed new—and genuine!— whenever Jasper performed it.

There was his slick, quick presentation of Oswald Williams's "Watch Your Watch," in which he told a story of a footpad who had stolen his watch, wrapped it in a handkerchief, and gone home. This was accompanied, of course, by the suitable actions. The watch was taken from his wrist, placed in the handkerchief and suddenly vanished. Pulling up his sleeve, Jasper would then show the watch back on his wrist. A very easy trick, indeed. But in Jasper Maskelyne's hands it was a masterpiece.

And of course there was his sparkling performance of that age-old classic of magic, the Chinese Linking Rings. Many amateur magicians speak with some scorn of Jasper's Linking Rings. "Altogether too simple, his method," they will say. But they are looking at this fine old trick from the point of view of the magician who wonders how difficult he can make a trick. If they had listened to the comments of the audience, they might well have taken a leaf out of Jasper's book and played the Linking Rings straight— and simple.

With variety theatres sadly depleted throughout the country, Jasper at last decided to achieve a lifelong ambition—he would leave the stage and be a farmer. His grandfather came of farming stock, and always Jasper had suffered an ardent yearning to return to the soil.

And so, it seemed, he was one day with us in London, where a Maskelyne had held the stage for seventy years and more, and the next day he was sailing for Kenya to buy a farm.

Somewhere in Africa today you'll find Jasper Maskelyne—*Farmer* Jasper Maskelyne—turning the African soil into rich bearing loam. And somewhere in Africa today, not far away from the Maskelyne farm, you'll find a store-house that contains many of the mysteries that Farmer Maskelyne loves almost as much as the soil. And, if you're especially lucky, Farmer Maskelyne might become Magician Maskelyne once more, and unlock his storehouse of magic.

If ever Farmer Maskelyne feels that a couple of years' holiday in London would do him good, London will give him the Prodigal Son's welcome, for his is still—a name to conjure with.

CHAPTER NINE

TOP OF THE BILL

IN the golden days of magic, when variety theatres stood side by side in the city streets where now stand the super-cinemas, you'd have been unlucky if at least one theatre in any given town didn't have a magician as top of the bill. Those were the days—the palmy days—when Chung Ling Soo was delighting theatre audiences throughout Britain with his colourful, mysterious, baffling show. Poor Soo! Springing to fame in Britain at forty years of age, after struggling along in America for the early part of his career, he was to see the Last Curtain fall in tragic circumstances. On March 23rd, 1918, he fell, mortally wounded, on the stage of the Wood Green Empire, while performing his dangerous bullet-catching trick. And when he died, the world learned that Chung Ling Soo, Mandarin of the One Button, was none other than New York-born Billy Robinson.

Soo had carried his mysteries into real life, and for nearly twenty years had made the world believe that he was a high-caste Chinese. But whether he was American-born or not, he will always remain Chung Ling Soo, the Marvellous Chinese Conjurer, to the magicians of the world.

Those were the days, too, when the remote, icy grandeur of Lafayette charmed the music-hall audiences. Lafayette, born Sigmund Neuberger in Germany, was another spectacular figure to die tragically. He met his end in a great theatre fire in Edinburgh. Lafayette, legend says, could have saved himself in the fire if he had not returned to the blazing theatre to save his dog, Beauty. When firemen first searched the charred, reeking wreckage of the theatre, they found an almost unrecognisable figure curled in the agony of death behind one of the backstage doors. Was it Lafayette? Or was it the man who played his double in some of the illusions? Even today there are students of magic lore who claim that the mystery was never solved to everyone's satisfaction. Be that as it may, Lafayette's tomb, bearing a marble figure of his dog, Beauty, is to be seen in Edinburgh today.

Lafayette toured a magical revue of the spectacular variety, emphasising colourful beauty in each scene. In private life he was a thoughtful, studious man, and his gold-rimmed pince-nez and dark clothes gave him a resemblance to a bank manager or a lawyer rather than a glittering star of the theatre. It was Lafayette who introduced the vogue for using living animals in illusions. In one of his famous scenes, Lafayette would ride on the stage upon a sleek, gleaming, snow-white horse. His dogs and other animals were his life, he used to say, and long before his death he issued instructions that his tomb was to bear the effigy of his dog and the inscription: "The more I see of men, the more I love my dog."

Into the shoes of Lafayette stepped Horace Goldin, an American magician of some fame. Goldin was a chubby, smiling little man, who shared with Lafayette the love of animals, and who used them frequently on the stage. One of his favourite illusions was a small-scale model of an experiment in which a girl would be passed through a giant mirror. Goldin would perform the illusion with one of his dogs, a tiny, smooth-haired Chihuahua. "Best little dog in the world!" Goldin would murmur, stroking the little dog as he set up the apparatus. And when the trick was over, there would be the tiny dog on the other side of the mirror, wagging his absurd tail delightedly at the success of the illusion—and in anticipation of the titbit that was always forthcoming from Goldin's pocket.

Who doesn't remember at least the name of Harry Houdini, the fearless stocky figure who escaped from the most appalling situations? Houdini—born Eric Weiss, the son of a Jewish rabbi in America—was a "natural" for the theatre from early youth. Tough, aggressive, agile, Houdini delighted in the publicity that challenges from the public brought him. He would escape from a strait-jacket while hanging upside down over the parapet of a New York skyscraper with the same apparent ease as he would get out of a cell in a British police station.

But Houdini had no supernatural powers, even though Sir Arthur Conan Doyle insisted that he could not perform his miracles without them. Houdini was merely a brilliant showman with a brain as keen as a razor. His escapes were achieved by two means: physical skill or secret collusion. The ability to escape from a strait-jacket—as today's leading escapologist Alan Alan will tell you—depends upon sheer muscular strength and agility. But to get out of a prison cell calls for something more than that.

In one of his most publicised escapes in Britain, Houdini was locked in a police cell. Before the key was turned, he was thoroughly examined with surgical minuteness by a team of doctors and police officers. One by one they certified that no secret key could possibly be hidden about Houdini's person. Then they shook hands with him and locked him in.

But still Houdini got out.

How?

The solution is absurdly simple, as are so many solutions to magical problems.

The last man to shake hands with Houdini was a confederate, who had hidden in his palm a duplicate key to the cell. The key changed hands secretly as the confederate murmured something like: "And the best of luck, Mr. Houdini!"

On another occasion Houdini was lowered through the ice of a frozen river, encased in a sealed box and firmly manacled. The incident was highlighted in the film of Houdini's life, but the secret was lost in a welter of Hollywood bathos. The film showed Houdini escaping from manacles and box, and then losing his way back to the hole in the thick ice. He was saved, according to the film, by hearing the voice of his dying mother direct him back to the hole in the ice, and in the meantime he managed to find enough oxygen to keep him breathing by swimming right up to the ice level, where a thin layer of air existed. The truth was very different, and involved the collusion of a deep-sea diver already stationed below the ice.

And, incidentally, his mother did not die for some years after that, and he actually heard of her death while travelling from New York to London by ship.

Houdini, always the aggressive challenger, met his death through a rash challenge. The film slipped sideways badly again in its treatment of his end, when it showed him battling to escape from a water-filled glass tank—and failing.

The facts were very different. Houdini had always taken pride in his physical perfection, and lost no opportunity of boasting of it. On one occasion he was addressing some college students in America and dwelt long and loudly on the theme of physical perfection. He could, he announced, withstand any blow to the body because he had trained the muscles that protected the abdomen. Suddenly, and without warning, a student launched a swift blow to Houdini's stomach. The muscles were not braced to receive the blow, and the resultant internal injuries were responsible for Houdini's death soon after.

Soo, Lafayette, Goldin, Houdini. More names to conjure with. Here were just four of the glamorous stars of the magical scene of the early years of the century. There were others—many others—but the list is too long to detail here. And then, in the years between the wars, there developed another style of magic.

It was introduced by a diminutive, white-suited page-boy, strolling across the stage and: "Paging Mr. Cardini! Paging Mr. Cardini!"

And from the wings a solemn, if rather uncertain on his feet, Mr. Cardini would peer at the audience before making his entrance. Things happened to Cardini. Things that were as inexplicable to him as to the audience. Fans of cards appeared at his finger ends. Billiard balls slowly but certainly multiplied themselves in his hands. Lighted cigarettes twinkled in mid-air as they appeared from nowhere to be clipped in his lips.

Cardini was the master and originator of the inebriated magical act. And Cardini was perfection. Here was pure sleight of hand allied to an acting ability of the highest order. Since then, hundreds of top-hatted, white-tied revellers have teetered across the stage and produced card fans, billiard balls and lighted cigarettes. But not one has had the makings of a Cardini.

The only two, to my mind, who brought originality to the foundation laid by Cardini were the late Willane, wealthy fruit-broker who established for himself a high reputation as a stage magician, and Douglas Francis, young Liverpool magician who was christened Douglas Jones. Francis is still with us, and his faultless card work is frequently seen at the Magic Circle.

But there was only one Cardini, though many sleight of hand conjurers added "-ini" to their names.

Cardini was a young Welshman who found his way to the top by the same means that have provided stepping-stones for so many other magicians —as salesman at Gamage's magical counter. Richard Pitchford was—and is —his real name. Even today, living in retirement in New York, Richard Pitchford Cardini retains the accent of the Welsh valleys. If you ever saw him perform at London's Palladium, you would not have known that Cardini was Welsh, for his act was performed in complete silence. The small page-boy who ushered him on stage was Mrs. Pitchford. Today, New York and the United States, bereft of vaudeville, occasionally see Cardini and Partner in cabaret or on television. But the audiences for whom he loves best to perform are those closely packed rows of magicians who assemble for the magical conventions. They claim to know every move—even to that cunning secret loading of a billiard ball when the monocle drops from his eye—but they rise and cheer him to the echo when the last card fan, the final cigarette, and the concluding billiard ball have appeared.

Cardini is, and rightly so, one of today's great heroes of all the world's magicians.

Cardini's polished suavity introduced a new theme to the stage. The flamboyant, spectacular wizards were gradually replaced by the sophisticated, smoothly efficient magicians of today.

Ingenuity of mechanical principle gave way to sheer digital skill and hypnotic powers of misdirection.

Where the great magi of the past had performed a full evening's show, or at least half of a variety bill, the 12-minute-spot man came into his own. Often, he performed alone, standing spotlighted in the centre of the stage.

I believe that in years to come the names of such performers will be headed in the archives of magic by one man—Robert Harbin. Harbin is the most versatile, the most diabolically inventive, and the most pleasing—to my mind—of all the solo performers. His magical inventions, many of them published in the magical Press, must run into hundreds. He will make up some complex effect and fearlessly perform it on television the next night. And then the masterpiece will be laid aside until someone reminds him about it again.

Harbin is another figure who appeared in Britain, as if by magic, between the wars. In his native South Africa he was Ned Williams, and for some years after arriving in Britain he worked under the same name. Young Ned Williams was another magician who spent his apprentice years behind Gamage's counter. The tricks he invented are still sold over that same counter, as well as in other dealers' shops. For a few shillings you may still buy "The Ned Williams Rope and Rings" trick, or one of a score of other of his creations—creations which he himself has no doubt forgotten by now, but which are none the less excellent value for that.

Ned Williams was advised to change his name by the Maskelyne and Devant combination. They had him earmarked for top billing at St. George's Hall, and there was already a Williams—Oswald Williams—who was famous as a magician. And so today there are few who call him by his own name. If you call "Ned!" across the Magic Circle clubroom, he won't look round. But try calling "Bob!" and you'll have his attention at once.

When the Duke of Edinburgh visited the Magic Circle, the first choice of a magician to entertain him naturally fell upon Robert Harbin. And it was Harbin who chattily asked His Royal Highness: "Have you ever sawn anyone in half, sir?" and inveigled the Duke on to the stage, there to take one end of the saw that was to saw his aide in half.

This sawing-in-half illusion of Harbin's must be seen to be believed—and even then you won't believe it! The victim, usually a young woman, is asked if she has ever been sawn in half, and assured that after the operation she'll feel twice the girl she was. She reclines on two chairs, and is thereupon operated upon with a gigantic Canadian lumber saw. At the end, the blade of the saw is beneath her and the frame is above her. What could be fairer than that? And even the victim (who receives a printed certificate to the effect that she is the 8,461st to be sawn in half) cannot tell you how it's done.

At the Magic Circle's annual Festival of Magic at the Scala Theatre in London in 1954, Harbin staged three never-to-be-forgotten illusions, in which he suspended a girl from the audience in mid-air without any support, sawed the same girl in half, and then, before the eyes of two thousand people, caused her *slowly* to vanish. Even the expert magicians left the theatre shaking their heads in mystification.

I had the privilege of seeing some of the backstage work on this last extraordinary vanishing trick of Harbin's, when he was building the apparatus. He spared no expense to acquire exactly the right equipment, and travelled many miles up and down the country to find the right craftsmen to provide the electrical and electronic gear. Not until he was completely satisfied that it could be achieved without danger to the subject or the audience would he consent to operate it. I could tell you of the long months of patient experimenting Harbin spent in the initial stages of this illusion, of the trial-and-error methods that gave way to intensive study of electronics, and of the final triumph when a dummy figure, placed in the heavily wired glass cabinet, at last vanished from our view.

But these are matters only to be written about in the secret archives of magic, and would convey little to the layman.

A book could be written with Robert Harbin as its sole subject. It could tell of his season as "The Wizard of Oz" in the West End production of that play, when the crazy wizardry—which never failed—was carried on between scenes in his dressing room. It could tell of his long career on the music-hall stage, of his slick cabaret work (surely the hardest places in which to perform magic are London's West End cabarets, where bored audiences have to be dynamited into paying attention!), of his copious writings for the magical Press. It could also tell of his infinite patience in small things, such as his trick in which he tears up a newspaper and then shakes it open to show it completely restored—and with no torn bits left! The trick occupies perhaps ninety seconds of time, but its perfection took Harbin many weeks of experimenting.

Radio and television have brought fame to many magical artistes, and their aid has been appreciated, probably, by none more than that amazing couple, the Piddingtons. Their story has already been told by Russell Braddon in the Piddingtons' biography he wrote, but there are many aspects of this likeable pair which are known only to their friends.

It was in Changi Jail, as a prisoner of war in the hands of the Japanese, that Sydney Piddington developed his ability to convey his thoughts over a distance. But even with the skill he and his wife, Lesley, knew they possessed, they came to London with some trepidation. Fortunately, they placed their affairs in the hands of a wise agent who appreciated their talents when he first saw them.

For a time things didn't seem to be going well for the Piddingtons. They were offered bookings, true, but the booking they wanted was still somewhere in the future—the booking by the BBC. They determined that, rather than struggle along with a few theatrical engagements, they would accept nothing until they had secured a broadcast.

And it was only when funds had run so low as to leave them with just their fare home to Australia that the BBC offered them a broadcast. This, they said to each other, was IT.

On the evening of July 7th, 1949, they went on the air. Sydney transmitted mentally a colour, Lesley successfully divined a geometrical pattern (although she drew it upside down on the blackboard), and they were away!

Then for the final test, Barrington Dalby, famous sports broadcaster, selected a line in a book. Blindfolded, Lesley Piddington hesitated. She shook her head slowly. The words would not come. The studio audience held its breath until—Lesley flashed into life and certainty. "The words seem to be . . . 'like a picture—an ugly picture—in the mind . . . in the mind of . . . a child!' " she said triumphantly.

Barrington Dalby nodded rapidly and delightedly. "Absolutely right!" he agreed.

And, in a few minutes, the Piddingtons had arrived!

Next morning the newspapers carried such headlines as: "THESE TELEPATHY TESTS CONVINCED ME"; "THE PIDDINGTONS' ACT IS A WINNER—HOW DO THEY DO IT?"; "DO WE REALLY KNOW ABOUT TELEPATHY?"; "PIDDINGTONS' SHOW HITS BBC AIR"; "THIS SHOW WORKS BY MENTAL TELEPATHY."

For months afterwards, the Piddingtons figured in the headlines, in the cartoons, in "Letters to the Editor," in learned scientific debate and in everybody's conversation.

As they toured the country after their broadcasts, they were beset by amateur magicians, often frantically jealous, who threatened to "expose" their methods. I was present at one such interview, in the Midlands, when two magicians claimed to "know how they did it."

"So what?" asked Sydney mildly. "We know how we do it, too. We don't need *showing* how we do it."

There was a threat. "Unless you tell us how you do it, we'll get up in the theatre tonight and tell everyone . . ."

"But surely," put in Lesley, sweetly, "if you're going to do that, you know how we do it. In which case, you don't require us to tell you how we do it!"

The affair ended with peace on all sides. The two amateur magicians demonstrated their powers, which were duly admired by the Piddingtons, and they attended the theatre that night and applauded with the rest of the audience.

And as I joined them later in their dressing room, Sydney whistled. "Phew!" he said. "This worry is getting me down!"

It wasn't the worry of having people know how they did it—their methods were very, very simple and straightforward—but the worry of a hitch in the show that troubled him and his wife. Together, they were keyed up to the ultimate limit at every performance, and a sudden shout from the audience would have broken up the show and probably brought on nervous breakdowns for both.

You will remember, no doubt, that they used to leave their audiences of the radio or theatre with the simple statement: "You are the judges!" Never did they make claims to possess any psychic powers or any ability that was not shared by the majority of other people. They had, however, one great ability that is rare—the ability to entertain. It goes by different names, this unusual talent. Sometimes it's called showmanship, sometimes it's "sense of theatre," sometimes it's "personality," sometimes it's "it." Whatever you call it, the Piddingtons had it.

They also had sound good commercial sense.

The last time I met them was at the Nottingham Empire. "This is the last time we shall play this circuit," said Sydney.

"Why?" I asked. "Going on that American tour?"

"No," he said. "We're going into business."

Now to theatrical folk there is "the" business, which means their own job in the theatre, and there is "business," which they sometimes pronounce with a wistful air, and by which they mean the strange outside world of buying and selling, plotting and planning, investing and collecting. It was in this latter sense that Sydney Piddington used the word.

"We're going into the publishing business," he told me. Then, anticipating my question, he added: "We're getting out of the theatre while we're on top. We feel that we're now on the crest of the wave . . . and we hate to think that tomorrow we might be on the way down."

And so quite suddenly, while they were at the height of their success, the Piddingtons went out—as suddenly as they'd come in, but with less publicity. If you want to see a demonstration of their powers today, you'd have to travel to Australia, where they have set up their home once again. You'd have to persuade housewife Lesley and business executive Sydney to drop their more homely interests. They might do it. I don't know. But this I do know: when Sydney and Lesley Piddington went back home to Australia and to private life, the theatre lost two wonderful artistes, and many of us who knew them lost—by distance, not by sentiment—two lovable friends.

Was it thought-reading? You'll still find people who'll debate the powers of the Piddingtons. Whether it was, or whether it was clever conjuring, they were magicians in the truest sense of the word. And they left us with those four words with which they always closed their act: "You are the judges!"

There's another fellow I'd like you to meet—another performer about whom the public have said: "It's just impossible!" He works with his hands in public, but for every minute of his performance on the stage he's spent many an hour of brainwork in his study.

If you live in Britain you may never have heard of him. But wherever you live, if you're a conjurer, his name will be almost a legend to you.

Dai Vernon was born in Canada, but has spent most of his sixty-odd years in the United States. There's another miracle that he can apparently perform: he looks thirty years younger, he acts thirty years younger, and unless you knew his age you'd swear that he *was* thirty years younger.

Dai is the conjurer *par excellence*. His magic baffles magicians. His methods are his own. The effects he procures are often unique. The tricks he adapts and makes over become new—and even more mystifying—magic.

Dai Vernon is probably the world's greatest authority on pure sleight of hand today. His fingers look just like your fingers or my fingers, but they can effect miracles of prestidigitation.

Harry Stanley, the well-known London magical dealer, did British magicians a great service when he brought Dai Vernon to this country on an extended lecture tour. I was fortunate enough to attend his first lecture, and it was an experience I shall never forget.

London's Victoria Hall, in Bloomsbury, was crowded to the doors with hundreds of magicians who had come from all over the country to hear what Maestro Dai Vernon had to tell them. An American friend had warned me beforehand: "Take a notebook and a stenographer. This guy Vernon will talk a blue streak. He'll show you how to do fifty tricks, one after the other. And you'll come away dizzy. Then when you want to recall just one thing he's shown you—you'll find you can't."

For hours Vernon spoke and demonstrated. He had two tricks I wanted to learn: a little thing in which four olives or marbles pass from one hand to the other imperceptibly, and his own version of the famous Thumb-Tie Trick, in which hoops are passed over the performer's arms even though his thumbs are firmly tied together.

Vernon started with the marble trick. When it was over, I stayed on, but let everything else go over my head. He finished with the thumb-tie trick. I came away with those two tricks, and Vernon's methods, firmly fixed in my mind. The sponsor of the lecture had thoughtfully provided printed notes of everything, but even so Vernon explained so many unscheduled items that many of us had to attend other lectures to get what we wanted. Many magicians, for the privilege of more private tuition, gladly paid £5 each for a session with Vernon, and would as gladly have paid much more for the invaluable information they received.

Yes, Dai Vernon is a unique character, blessed with the combination of a keen brain and unparalleled dexterity.

I wanted to tell you about Vernon so that you might have some insight into the intense interest in magical education to be found among conjurers. A course of Vernon is just about equal, in the magical world, to a university degree.

From an unknown name to a household word. From Dai Vernon, the incomparable instructor, to Tommy Cooper, the king of crazy conjurers.

You think it's easy, this madcap magic as practised by Tommy Cooper? Listen to Tommy discussing the introduction of a new trick into his programme. Watch his thoughtful appraisal of a new idea. Eavesdrop on him as he searches the magical depots for something that will give a new twist to an idea he has. Tommy Cooper offstage is a keen businessman. His business is crazy conjuring. His assets are that wild, wild look, that long lank hair, and an exquisite sense of timing.

I remember the first time Tommy Cooper performed before the Magic Circle. Carefully setting up his little table on the tiny stage in the old clubroom at St. Ermin's Hotel, he started off by dropping something. He picked it up, looked at it with horror, and thrust it rapidly back into his attaché case. The next item he wanted wasn't there, so he went on to something else. The audience laughed. Tommy glared balefully at them— and then split our eardrums with that eldritch screech of his that he calls a laugh. In an instant his face was straight again. He rummaged in his attaché case for this and that, he dropped nearly everything in turn, he talked, he rolled his eyes madly, he swept from side to side of the stage in a fine dramatic frenzy when thwarted.

To this day we don't know whether he'd rehearsed it all or whether he was kidding us that he was a conjurer. But *how* we laughed!

Now Tommy Cooper is a big star, and deservedly so. But whenever he has an hour to spare on a Monday night he'll visit his old friends at the Magic Circle, where he'll put on an act such as was never seen in the West End theatres where most of his work is now done.

This six-foot-something zany wasn't always a comedy conjurer. It's an act that's been developed since the war. When he left the Guards, with whom he saw service in the Western Desert, Tommy Cooper was determined to make a name for himself in the theatre. How well he's succeeded everybody knows.

Undoubtedly television helped to make Tommy Cooper's kind of magic popular. And it was television that introduced to millions of viewers all over the country another magician—David Nixon. But please don't think that David Nixon wouldn't have got to the top without TV. He was getting along very nicely before the BBC thought that he'd make a good panel member.

After all, David was no beginner in the world of entertainment when he first appeared in "What's My Line?" For years he'd been appearing at London's leading cabarets, and had been a prominent society entertainer with a full diary of bookings. It seems odd that when his fame began to spread on a nation-wide scale it was as a panel member on television. But David Nixon is still a magical entertainer, and as such television is now making more use of him.

Born in 1919, this gentle-voiced, gentlemanly trickster learnt the art of pleasing bigger audiences as a member of that famous concert party, the Folderols. The character he portrays on the stage—the confidential, eager, friendly chap with a couple of tricks he's dying to show—is his own. He's not playing a part on the stage—he's playing David Nixon. But don't get the idea that because he may sometimes seem a silly-ass type on stage he's like that in private life. Here is an artiste who has all his wits about him always. His sudden access to wider popularity didn't altogether take him by surprise. In his own sphere as a society entertainer he'd always held a high place. His former audiences and associates weren't the least bit astonished when their old friend David Nixon became a star of national magnitude, and neither was Nixon. Not that he held exalted ideas about his abilities. He simply saw himself at his true value. He knew what he was capable of doing, and he did it well.

Now, thanks to television, every viewer knows what he's capable of doing, and David Nixon is established as a star in two galaxies at the same time—in the glittering sphere of society entertainment and in the wider sphere of television.

I would say that David Nixon's greatest attribute is his uncanny knowledge of correct timing. Try repeating one of his jokes yourself. Somebody may laught at it, or may not. Then ask yourself why *you* thought it so hilariously funny when you heard it from Nixon. Listen to him again and note the pauses he makes, the slow casting of an eye round the audience, the thoughtful tongue-tip at the corner of the mouth now and then, the all-embracing smile at some stage of the story. These natural aids to timing and pointing *are* natural in his case (though that doesn't say he hasn't studied them and their effect carefully). But in the case of many another entertainer they'd be carefully rehearsed, and wouldn't quite bear the stamp of authenticity Nixon brings to them.

David Nixon is a natural-born entertainer, and it doesn't seem possible to imagine him in any other field of activity. Magicians are thankful that David combines entertaining with magic. We wish, too, that more amateur magicians would do the same.

Another professional magician who recognises to the full the need for entertainment in magic is Benson Dulay, "The Sorcerer and his Apprentices."

Benson Dulay has been touring the British music-halls for years under this style, and in that time has evolved a show that is outstanding for its high entertainment value. And yet it's full of mystery as well. Always an expert conjurer, Benson combines his skill with that of a fine craftsman (for years he was one of the most sought-after builders of illusions for the big illusionists) and the accomplished visual wit of an international entertainer. Much of his comedy business, he will tell you, he learnt while he worked with the Olsen and Johnson Show, *Hellzapoppin*. But that's modesty. His quick brain can assess the possibilities of a comedy situation even while he's only planning it.

I once took Benson Dulay on a surprise visit to the editor of a daily newspaper. The two had been boys together in Northampton. The editor was no theatregoer, and had not seen his old friend for many years. When they met, the editor held out a delighted hand.

"Well! If it isn't Billy Dooley!" he exlaimed. "Where have you been all these years? What are you doing these days?"

Benson Dulay, christened William Dooley, confessed modestly that he was working at the theatre across the road. I had to break the news to the editor that Billy Dooley was now Benson Dulay, and that the queue then forming outside the theatre was lining up to see his top-of-the-bill act.

"I'm not a bit surprised!" confessed the editor. "Remembering what a joker you were at school, I just couldn't imagine you doing any other job."

The fun that Benson Dulay extracts from his two "assistants from the audience" has to be seen to be believed. So well coached are the two youths, that few audiences will believe they are anything but casual members of the audience—until the climax of this riotous act, when those who have not laughed tears into their eyes may begin to wonder what's happened to the two boys after all this.

But Benson Dulay doesn't depend upon confederacy for his effects. He tours one of the neatest and most baffling levitation illusions I have ever seen, built, of course, in his own Northampton workshops. A levitation is a bulky thing to travel with, but Benson's can be packed into the back of a car The "works" are a closely guarded secret which many magicians would give a lot to have explained to them.

As well as his comedy scena, Benson Dulay always shows two or three major illusions of his own creation, and these are always worth seeing for their technical purity. In these days of intimate entertainment, creative inventors of illusions are rare, and Benson Dulay, born William Dooley, is carrying on the traditions of the great masters of magic in his music-hall work.

In the amateur and semi-professional field, illusionists—as compared with conjurers performing smaller effects—are rare. The outstanding example of such performers today is Reg Salmon, whose illusions have frequently been seen on television, as well as in variety theatres and cabarets around London.

Reg Salmon, by daytime, is managing director of one of the world's biggest news photograph agencies. By night he is an illusionist on the grand scale. He's a modest fellow, this businessman-magician. "The girls do all the work in my show," he'll tell you. "I'm only the chap who does the talking."

That may be so. It's nearly always the assistants who do the work in illusions with living people. But it's the illusionist himself who plans, builds, and produces the show. There's a lot of brainwork and building behind even the simplest illusion. You want to make a lady vanish from a box? Nothing easier—provided you know how to build the box. You've built the box? Good. Now find yourself an intelligent girl of exactly the right size, not only to get into the box, but to get *out* of it. An inch too big one way, and the lady will stick in the box. You have a girl who can get into and out of the box? Fine. Now start thinking about angles. Can you set up your illusion in the middle of a ballroom floor? Must it have a raised platform? Do you have to ensure that nobody stands behind it? Do you need somebody else—seen or unseen—to get your lady out of the box? What about special lighting?

These are just a few of the scores of questions for which the illusionists must have an answer.

I once knew an amateur illusionist who built the most baffling vanishing lady illusion. There was one great drawback to it: it couldn't be performed without a stage fitted with traps and a special counterbalance system in the flies. My friend's magical engagements were confined to concert work. The nearest theatre that could accommodate his illusion was thirty miles away, and was *never* leased for one-night concerts. To this day, as far as I know, that marvellous illusion is gathering dust in my friend's garage.

And so the interested amateur has to give thought to many aspects of presentation that don't face the full-time professional working regularly in fully equipped theatres. More—he has to be able to transport his often massive equipment for many miles. His illusions, therefore, must be designed and made for quick setting and striking, easy transport, and presentation almost anywhere, from a fitted stage to a field at a garden party.

That's why I admire the work of illusionists like Reg Salmon, who can work in a variety theatre or a drawing room with equal ease and efficiency. There are few of them nowadays, but wherever you see them they are truly "Top of the bill."

Oddly enough, "Top of the bill" quite often means "bottom of the bill," for the name of the star performer in a variety theatre is frequently printed below all the rest—although in bigger type—on the playbill.

And so it's fitting that this chapter should close by listing last of all the greatest showman of all—Kalanag.

Kalanag is a German magician who today travels the biggest magical revue there is. He is one of the few performers whose show is of such magnitude that it's booked for two-week stands in English provincial theatres, instead of the more usual one week in each town.

There are tons of scenery, equipment and billboard matter in the Kalanag show. There are thirty or forty members of the company, recruited from all over the world. One member of Kalanag's troupe never appears on the stage. He is a chemist, whose work is confined to one trick only, which must be specially prepared for each show. I don't propose to tell you which trick employs this man for a full day's work six days a week, but no doubt if you've seen the show you can form your own opinion.

Kalanag—real name Helmut Schreiber—is a jovial, portly figure in his fifties, with all the zest and agility of a man half the age. From start to finish his show goes with a ZIP! which most other magicians have found impossible to imitate or duplicate. You feel breathless when the final curtain swings down, and you'll go away from the theatre and remember Kalanag for the rest of your days.

That's showmanship!

Kalanag has his own studios and theatrical workshops in Hamburg, where his illusions are built—and often rebuilt time and time again in the search for perfection—and rehearsed before being taken out on tours that may embrace half the world.

In between travelling his show throughout Europe, Africa, and the Dominions, Kalanag and his partner, Gloria de Voss, have found time to learn the languages of each country they perform in. Hear him in London's Stoll Theatre, where he played for a long season when first the show came to Britain, and you'd say he was an Englishman who'd perhaps lived abroad for some years. Then hear him in Zurich's Corso-Theater, and you'd say he was Schweitzer-Deutsch. Italians in Rome understand his Italian better than they understand some of their own dialects, and I'd be prepared to wager that his Afrikaans, when showing in South Africa, is of text-book standard.

Watch him present his wonderful levitation of a living person, against a bizarre but beautiful background of a heathen temple. See him cock his eye quickly over the house, and smile gleefully for a second. That's because he knows that his secret method of raising a person from the ground will always be a secret. There just *couldn't* be any concealed wires or supports in Kalanag's method, you'll say! When Kalanag does the levitation illusion, it's real magic—or the nearest thing to magic you're ever likely to see in this practical world.

Everything Kalanag does is done on the majestic scale. In April, 1955, when the Magic Circle celebrate its golden jubilee, Kalanag insisted on coming over from Germany just to perform "a trick or two" at the final Gala Night show.

What happened? Around the middle of the afternoon, an air-liner glided to rest at London Airport. Out of it came Kalanag and Gloria—followed by thirty members of his company!

They put on a whirlwind potted version of their famous magical revue, presented at lightning speed. When the curtain came down, the great audience rose to its feet and gave Kalanag a standing ovation. Back came Kalanag, Gloria, and the company. And *they* gave something in return—a heavy silver pitcher, beautifully inscribed, for the Magic Circle museum.

Why a silver pitcher?

"Water from India!" is the answer.

If you've seen Kalanag's show, you'll know about "Water from India!" It's what's known in the theatrical world as a running gag. Right through the evening's show, from time to time, and with solemn ritual, Kalanag pours water from a single small pitcher into buckets on the stage. That one pitcher, holding perhaps a quart when full, yet provides enough water to fill many buckets. And each time Kalanag pours out another quart of water, he tells you gravely and dramatically that it's "Water—from India!"

Where does it all come from? Never once does the pitcher leave the sight of the audience, you'd be prepared to swear. And yet it's always full. Yet, do you know, if you examined that pitcher, or the silver one in the Circle's museum, you'd find them both quite free from any suspicious preparation.

When Kalanag had finished his one-night show specially for the Magic Circle, he and his company packed up, rushed out to the waiting airport bus, and were flying back to Germany before the final curtain came down on the Gala performance.

Houdini used to make an elephant disappear on the stage. The animal was led into a large cage on wheels (it took two men to push the cage on to the stage) and suddenly it would vanish. The cage would then be wheeled off stage (and it took eight men to wheel it off—now can you work it out?)

If Kalanag vanished an elephant, you'd probably see the animal walking down the aisle from the back rows at the moment it vanished. He'd certainly never commit the error of allowing the "cage" to be seen heavier at the finish than it was at the start.

As it is, Kalanag makes a motor car vanish before the eyes of the audience —a motor car containing Gloria and perhaps a reporter or a member of the audience. One moment the car's there before your eyes, and then—SIM SALA BIM!—it's gone. The mechanism needed to achieve this startling illusion weighs several tons, and is insured for some thousands of pounds. And yet it's all there on the stage for you to see. It's a perfect illusion, and I commend it to you as the ideal lesson in the magic of illusion. All that's needed to make the motor car vanish, is there before your eyes.

But when you've sat through the Kalanag show you simply won't *believe* your eyes!

I know magicians who've visited the theatre where Kalanag has been performing, not once but for every night of the run. If that isn't praise I don't know what is!

And if Kalanag's conjuring isn't magic, I don't know what is!

So with that salute to the Master Magician of our time, let's leave this gallery of Tops of the Bill. We leave it a little thoughtfully, for there are many names we haven't been able to include, many fine magicians who deserve their place as Top of the Bill, and many, many young artistes who will undoubtedly, in their day, be as bright and glittering stars as any who ever shone at the Top of the Bill.

CHAPTER TEN

THEY MAKE THE MAGIC

SECRETIVE chaps, these magicians. They'd as soon jump in the river as tell you how their miracles are performed. Rightly, too. For if you once knew *all* their secrets, half the fun of watching the magician would be gone. Gone, that is, unless you are one of those ardent enthusiasts who derive as much pleasure from appraising technique as from puzzling how it's done.

But there's one class of magical enthusiasts who *do* disclose their secrets—but only for the benefit of their fellow magicians. These are the back-room boys, the ones who plot and plan and sell the magic. As likely as not, they may be only moderately good performers themselves (for designing skill and performing ability don't always go together) but they are none the less dedicated to the magic arts, for all that. Indeed, they are the true devotees, often fostering their consuming interest in magic purely from love of their subject, whereas the professional performer has another motive—his career.

The back-room boys are the ones who provide the conjurer with the tools of his trade. They are the ones who sit night after night at the kitchen table, surrounded by an awesome pile of debris. Playing cards litter their waking hours, subtle principles occupy their every thought, delicate mechanisms hide in their bureau drawers, and ever beside them stalks the phantom of the ultimate mystery awaiting solution.

Their names are seldom known to the public, but to the conjurer theirs are the names to conjure with.

For example, it would mean nothing to the layman to learn that a particular piece of apparatus might have been made by Martin. Martin? Martin? There are thousands of Martins. But to the magician there is only one Martin. Today he is almost a legendary figure, able to command almost any price he names for the marvellous mechanisms he produces.

There's a famous trick—you *must* have seen it, often—known as the Rising Cards. There are literally hundreds of ways of performing the Rising Cards. You might use a thread, cunningly concealed and operated, to make the chosen cards rise from the pack. You might use . . . But we're getting on dangerous ground. It's sufficient to say that Martin makes one version of the Rising Cards. Before the war, you could have bought Martin's version for perhaps five to ten pounds. Today, if you can persuade him to make one for you, you might pay ten times that amount. A lot of money? So it is, but it's worth it, to the practising conjurer.

An American magician who is a friend of mine coveted, above all things, a Martin Pack. In America he combed the market. There were Martin Packs there, to be sure, but no owner would sell. In Britain I sought a Martin Pack that might be for sale, from end to end of the country. Nobody would sell. The American magician decided that only one thing was to be done. He must come to England and persuade Martin to make him a Martin Pack.

And he did. Dropping everything, he flew over, saw Martin, laid the money on Martin's work-bench, extracted a solemn promise of delivery in six months, and sailed back to America, content.

Six months later I shipped that Martin Pack to him, specially packed and heavily insured. That piece of mechanism had cost my friend possibly £400 in fares and other payments. But—he's more than content. He now owns one of the fabulous Martin Packs.

Examine the cards, and you'll find they're exactly like other cards, unless you know the secret. And you'll never even suspect the secret from the cards a Martin Pack owner will put in your hands.

Martin, who is a cunning worker in small mechanisms, makes other things. A Martin Finger Reel is a thing to be treasured. A Martin Bird Cage is a rare and costly piece of apparatus that the owner will never part with, once he's acquired one. And Martin's Ring Boxes, in beautifully engraved silver, with their minute secret mechanisms, are today veritable museum pieces of the craftsman's art.

Martin is the back-room boy above all back-room boys. His workmanship is superb, and his products, individually made to each magician's order, rarely change hands, for they are all but irreplaceable. And yet, to the best of my knowledge, Martin is no conjurer. But many magicians would as soon be without their right hand as without their Martin-made apparatus.

For many years, Martin has planned and made the mechanical mysteries of the great magicians. You've seen the results achieved by his workmanship many times. But unless you are the trusted friend of the owner of one of his pieces, you've never seen the actual work of Martin's hands.

Come to that, very, very few magicians have ever seen Martin. His whereabouts are known to none but a tiny handful of magicians. And in keeping with the secrecy of his work for magicians is the work he does for Government departments on top-secret mechanisms.

You've never heard of Martin until now? Of course you haven't. But his name is known to every magician who has studied his art.

We were talking about the Rising Cards a moment ago. There are many ways of performing this ancient trick, and one of the most practicable—and most easily available—comes in at the other end of the price scale. Where Martin can command £50 or more for his version, you can go into almost any magical dealer's shop and buy *this* version for as little as thirty shillings.

It started soon after the war, when Louis Histed, an official of the British Customs and Excise Department, published one of his many articles in magical magazines. The article described a new—quite new—method of making the cards rise from the pack. Histed called it "The Victory Rising Cards." The secret (there's no harm in revealing it now) depended upon a secret pendulum arrangement. The idea was good, as all of Louis Histed's ideas are good, but it had one drawback for the perfectionist: it used a piece of apparatus that *looked* like a piece of apparatus. And that is a big drawback.

However, another Customs and Excise official, who had also been badly bitten with the magic bug years ago, and whose name is Harry Mitchell, played with the idea for a time and worked out a near-perfect way of adapting it to more general use. Mitchell, whose stage name is Devano, and who, though a magical inventor of great ingenuity, is an exception to the planner-or-performer-but-not-both rule, did away with the odd-looking bit of apparatus needed for Histed's method. Mitchell's method used only the one pack of cards: nothing else.

He made up a few of his packs and tentatively took them along to a magical dealer. Within a week they were sold, and more—lots more—were being demanded by magicians who had seen the few trial packs.

Today the Devano Rising Cards are known throughout the whole world, and must have been performed before baffled audiences many thousands of times.

I know of a witch doctor (a member of the Magic Circle!) in Africa who has a Devano Pack. In Singapore there is a Chinese school teacher, a magician in his spare time, who has several of Devano's Packs. Hugo Adler, a ship's officer who sails the Seven Seas, carries three or four Devano Packs, to be on the safe side, and has shown their mystery to night-club audiences and to head-hunters' jamborees. Every magical dealer in the world, pretty well, carries the Devano Pack as part of his stock.

I'm not lucky enough to possess a Martin Pack, but I have two Devano packs, and until a Martin Pack comes my way I'm satisfied—at thirty bob a time.

There, then, are three of the back-room boys of magic. A watchmaker and two Customs and Excise men: three typical people who provide the magic that the conjurer performs. There are hundreds more—Peter Warlock, Brian MacCarthy, Ken de Courcy, Gil Leaney, Jack Hughes, and Lewis Ganson are just half a dozen of the many in Britain alone.

What happens to their tricks, in between their invention and creation, and their appearance on the stage or before the TV cameras?

This is where the magical dealer comes into the picture.

For the magical dealer is the man who has the ability to spot a clever trick, and the organisation to manufacture it. He knows the market for such things, and holds the stocks to supply the market. And believe me, he must have the space—and plenty of it—to store his mysterious stocks. This last qualification is a necessary one, when you consider that the apparatus for a single illusion often requires storage space the size of a private garage to house it. At the other end of the scale, you might fill a vest pocket with fifty tricks. Indeed, Edward Victor, that prolific magical inventor and fine sleight of hand expert, markets "Twenty Tricks in a Matchbox"—a literally truthful description.

Where are these magical dealers?

There must be half a hundred of them scattered throughout Britain, ranging from the tobacconist's shop that might stock a few jokes and pocket tricks to the store dealing exclusively in goods for magicians.

London alone has a dozen or so magical dealers, as you will know if ever you were a schoolboy in that city. What London boy does not know, for example, that famous den of magic in New Oxford Street, where an old-fashioned mirror sign over the door tells the passing world that this is "Davenports' Magic Shop"? What schoolboy has never heard of, and bought from, Gamage's or Hamley's conjuring departments?

These are some of the magic shops that welcome public business— although, if you seek to buy the inner secrets without being able to prove your fitness to possess them, you might be disappointed.

There are other dealers not so well known to the world, but whose names are bywords in the world of magic.

Up several flights of stairs in London's Archer Street, for example, you will find bearded Max Andrews and his staff of skilled craftsmen, anxious to provide the magician with everything magical, from a handkerchief trick to the apparatus for sawing a lady—*any* lady!—in half.

Without leaving Soho, and by merely walking through to Frith Street, you will find Harry Stanley's Unique Magic Studio, where, on Saturday afternoons, you may meet a dozen or so famous miracle workers, foregathered to swop tricks and gossip, and sometimes to buy. In the Unique Studio you may sit in an armchair and see the mysteries you propose to buy demonstrated to you from the studio's miniature stage, under complete stage conditions. This, as any magician will tell you, is a valuable aid to consideration.

At Gamages' you will find several counters packed and laden with the most tantalising things for the conjurer. Boxes and cylinders, handsomely coloured or polished to a high lustre, whose use is apparent to the initiate but which defy description by the novice, sit side by side with packs of cards whose designations—Brainwave, Stripper, Trilby, Mene Tekel, Nudist, Rough and Smooth, Mephisto—are everyday terms in the vocabulary of magic, however abstruse they may seem to the layman.

And the genial Harry Baron, manager of the department, will perform these miracles for you right before your very eyes on the counter's top, should you ask him to do so. And still they will remain mysteries to you, which is the highest commendation that can be bestowed on any trick or performer.

Go down into the basement of Hamley's famous toyshop in Regent Street, and in one corner you will meet Victor Fabian and his staff, behind still more glass counters packed with magical props, side by side with glittering showcases holding the more elaborate mysteries.

In side streets and main roads elsewhere throughout London and the provinces you will find the magical dealers, although "find" may not always be quite the correct word. Many of them are stowed away in deep, secret basements, in lofty, remote attics, in quiet private houses, with little or no advertisement to tell the passer-by that here are wonders to be seen.

If you can spare the time on some Saturday morning, and if you can make yourself inconspicuous almost to the point of invisibility, come with me to visit one of these magical dealers. We'll go along New Oxford Street to Davenports. This is where you'll find the true Bohemian atmosphere, as well as the veritable material of magic.

Over its fifty-seven years of existence, the Davenport business has spent most of its time along that short stretch of New Oxford Street bounded by Kingsway and Shaftesbury Avenue. Number 35 is its present home.

You'll find the shop, if by no other means, by the crowd round its windows, which are packed with tricks, small illusions, and "jokes."

Some years ago, the enterprising Davenport brothers nearly stopped the traffic in this busy main thoroughfare by displaying a Flying Saucer in the window. A genuine, sure-enough Flying Saucer—of the tea-table variety. It spun and swooped in the window without any visible means of support. It's still a secret, and the Davenports will never sell that secret.

But the real mysteries are inside the shop, so let's go in. The door-bell tinkles out a tinny peal that reminds us more of a village grocer's shop than an internationally famous business house. It's crowded inside, and likely to be noisy with chatter, too. Never mind about pushing through to the counter; just stand in this corner and watch—and listen.

When you feel that you can begin to concentrate on one thing at a time, and can forget all the wonderful and weird things in the showcases and on the shelves, look around you at the customers.

This chap in the middle of the group over here, tweed-coated, tousle-haired, and speaking with a soft Ulster brogue, is Billy McComb. If you frequent the glossier West End night clubs you may have seen McComb before, for he is an entertainer who specialises in the arduous technique of the floor show. He might have been William McComb, M.D., M.R.C.S., by now, but the lure of the spotlight once cast some sort of spell over him which has never abated, and medical student McComb became magician McComb some years ago. And if the McComb himself isn't familiar to you, his enchanting wife June surely must be. For June is also a magician, and, in addition, her action pictures are among the top priorities of Fleet Street's art editors.

At the moment, McComb is expounding on something they seem to call the Five Ring Routine.... Ah! Here's enlightenment being passed over the counter now, in the shape of eight large steel rings. Carefully McComb lays aside three of them, and demonstrates three minutes of wizardry with the remaining five. In his hands they link, unlink, pass from ring to ring, link and unlink again, until a round of applause tells us that McComb has convinced his little audience that you *can* perform the Linking Rings with five rings instead of the more usual eight or nine.

Now the talk centres round a young man with prematurely grey hair that gives him an air of some distinction. This is Al Koran—yes, you've seen him on television haven't you? And if you wondered whether his thought-reading was faked on TV, now you may have a chance to see it at close quarters, with little chance of any tricky work by the cameras.

Koran used to be a West End hairdresser of some repute. But here again, the spell of magic, combined with a keen brain and inventive genius, drew him into the wider world of entertainment. Today, he's known to theatre, cabaret and television audiences all over the country for his brilliant performances of mental magic.

What's he doing now, with that slip of paper, folded into a tiny package? Someone, while we've been talking, has written a message on it, afterwards folding it carefully, so that Al Koran can have no idea of what's been written. But even so, Koran, holding the paper at finger-tips and at arm's length, is slowly and hesitantly describing every word written on the paper. He looks up. "Is that right?" he asks the writer of the message.

"Absolutely right," says the other. "But—you got one word wrong."

"What do you think I am? A magician?" asks Koran, smiling as he tosses the paper slip, still folded, back to the writer for checking.

Something odd seems to be going on over in that other corner. A little dapper fellow with wavy black hair is having his hands tied together with a piece of rope. You're right—anything seems to happen in this place. It's Alan Alan we're watching now, whose theatre-bill matter describes him as "Escapologist." Now his wrists are firmly tied behind his back—quite, quite firmly. Go ahead, put an extra knot in the rope yourself. Make sure he's tied fast.

Alan turns to face us, and grimaces. "You surely tied that tightly," he agrees. From his breast pocket he takes out a silk handkerchief to mop his forehead. "I doubt whether I can get out of this," he says, putting the handkerchief back in his pocket and resuming his struggles. . . . But wait a minute! How did he get that hand free to mop his face?

"What hand?" he asks, turning his back to us again, so that we can see . . . both wrists firmly and securely tied.

There's a murmur of approval from the little crowd. The Kellar Wrist Tie (that's what you've just seen demonstrated) isn't often performed these days, and comparatively few magicians know the secret of it.

"You'll have to untie it," says Alan, with a sigh. "I'm afraid it's beaten me."

And as you untie the firm knots, and see the deep grooves the rope has cut in Alan's wrists, you begin to doubt whether you *did* see a hand pop out from behind Alan's back to take a handkerchief from his pocket. And if you did see a hand, whose was it? You may well ponder that riddle.

But we came in here to discuss the business of dealing in magical secrets, not to watch a series of impromptu performances. Come over here to the counter, now that the crowd has thinned somewhat.

This is George Davenport behind the counter. The world of magic, however, knows him as "Gilly" owing to his habit of murmuring "Gilly Gilly!" as a kind of spell when he is performing his magic.

Dark, bespectacled, always blue-suited and smoking a cigarette, George Davenport is around fifty years old, although to those who've been visiting the shop for the past thirty years or so he doesn't seem to have aged a day. That's probably another secret that he won't sell.

Mr. Davenport might well be called "Mr. Magic," for he knows all the magicians (and all their secrets) of the past fifty years and more.

He's been brought up in this curious world of "now you see it, now you don't," for his father and mother were prominent magical performers when he was born.

Back in 1898 Lewis Davenport, even in those days a magician of considerable renown, took a little shop opposite the People's Palace in the Mile End Road, there to sell magic books and tricks. Before long, the business had expanded so greatly that new premises were needed, and he moved into the New Oxford Street district, where a warehouse behind his new shop provided room for his growing stock. As the years passed, the business was transferred from shop to shop along New Oxford Street, still growing, still advancing. The warehouse overflowed, and another was rented. That grew too small in turn, and was extended.

Today, the Davenport business embraces the shop in New Oxford Street, storerooms behind and above and below it, Will Goldston's old studio off Leicester Square, the crypt of a blitzed church in Kingsway, and a disused Town Hall in a Kent town. There may well be other warehouses, too, for all I can tell you.

This is the biggest business of its kind in the world, although you might not suspect it, standing in this small, rather unimposing shop. In the Davenport warehouses are stored miracles of a past age, besides all the magical ingenuities of today—and probably tomorrow as well. Whole storehouses are given over to apparatus that once belonged to famous performers of a bygone day. Underground rooms are filled with crates containing apparatus that has not yet seen the light of day. The crypt round the corner in Kingsway is a never-failing topic of enchantment to magicians. "If only Gilly would open up some of those crates in the crypt," they sigh, exchanging opinions about the never-yet-seen mysteries that will some day come to light.

"But we just haven't the *time*," protests George Davenport. "With all this stock, stored all over the place, and with the business to run, and the mail order business to cope with, I never get a chance to sort out new lines on any scale. Mind you, I'd like to be able to open up the lot, and let our customers take their pick. Some day, maybe, I'll do that. . . ."

It's a family business today, is the Davenports'. Lewis Davenport, alas, is in failing health, and now seldom comes to London. His sons George, Gus and Wally handle the shop, the mail order trade (which is truly enormous) and the stock-keeping respectively. Until recently, George's daughters Jean and Betty used to help in the shop, until one of them took up nursing as a career. Now only her sister is to be seen behind the counter.

A big part of the business is taken up with the jokes and novelties beloved by schoolboys—and businessmen. But magic is the true heart of Davenports. Whether you buy a half-crown trick over the counter, or whether you have the Davenports build you the most elaborate illusion, running into the hundreds of pounds in cost, you'll get expert attention and advice.

Behind the counter in this little shop you'll see nests of drawers labelled with the most curious inscriptions—"Fly Paddles," "Atomic Vase," "Conradi Rope Fakes," "Wordo," "Demon Rod and Beads" and the like. The Demon trademark, by the way, is stamped on nearly everything you buy from Davenports. There are demon heads in the window, and a massive bronze statue of a demon at one end of the counter.

Inside the glass counters, safely out of reach of prying customers, are more mysteries by the score. The glass showcases that frame one wall contain the bigger stuff, from floating skulls to talking toby jugs, from Indian lota bowls to Chinese guillotines. And if there's not a crate or two, still being unpacked, on the floor in the middle of the shop, then we've struck a quiet day at Davenports.

But Saturday, the day of our visit, is never a quiet morning. In between talking to us, shouting down an old-fashioned speaking tube to the mysterious basement storeroom staff, quelling the argumentative magicians, dealing with a traveller or so, and putting money into the till, George Davenport has work to do before closing time at one o'clock.

So if you're ready, we'll leave him to it, and leave the chattering conjurers at one end of the shop and the eager schoolboys in search of stink bombs and black-face soap at the other end. And as we come out into New Oxford Street again, you may now add to your private memories the memory of a visit to this Demon's Den, this bazaar of mystery, this treasury of magic.

But the greatest magic of all, you may think, is how the magical dealers ever extract any sense out of their crazy stock—and their sometimes crazier customers.

CHAPTER ELEVEN

THE BOOKS OF MAGIC

THE literature of conjuring is, like Sam Weller's knowledge of London, both extensive and peculiar.

Peculiar? Well, you can't wonder at that!

But extensive? That may surprise you. Yet there are collections in which the books and booklets on magic are numbered in thousands. The reason for this is that most conjuring books are issued by specialist publishers who confine their sales to the magical fraternity. Indeed, some of the works are so highly technical that their general sale would be negligible, and their appeal to the public nil.

This specialised publication leads to a restricted market, which, in turn, has the disadvantage of forcing the price of conjuring books so high as to be almost excessive in many cases.

The major part of conjuring literature consists of books, booklets and brochures dealing with various aspects of magic. There are, also, the magical periodicals, which are dealt with in a separate chapter. Trade catalogues, programmes and manuscripts may also be of interest, although the literary value of many may be small. Conjuring articles from general magazines, and newspaper cuttings of a similar nature, may well fall within the scope of conjuring literature. It has, too, its own bibliographies, both general and national, and even boasts a bibliography of bibliographies (*Magical Bibliographies*, V. Farelli and J. B. Findlay, 1953).

What is the oldest piece of conjuring literature?

The question—which is almost impossible to answer with certainty—is a constant source of debate among the academically minded magicians.

Before the war there existed, in the Berlin State Museum, an Egyptian manuscript known as the Westcar Papyrus. This dated from about 1700 B.C., and described a magician's performance before King Khufu, or Cheops, some thousand years earlier. Among other marvels, a goose was decapitated and its head was joined to the body again—a trick which is still occasionally seen in foreign countries to this day.

Passing references to conjuring are to be found in the works of Chaucer, and Shakespeare makes numerous references to it. The earliest books on the subject appeared about a century after the invention of printing from movable type. In 1552 there appeared an anonymous work, attributed to Gilbert Walker, entitled *A Manifest Detection of Dice Play*. This gave a lengthy exposition on cheating at dice, and described card-sharping methods, some of which are still employed for conjuring—and card-sharping—purposes. Another edition appeared about 1580, and the work was reprinted in 1850.

In 1556 was published T. Hill's *Natural and Artificial Conclusions*, a book of what we would now call parlour magic and scientific recreations. Further editions were published in 1570, 1581, 1584, and later years, proving that the public taste for trickery was avid even in those days. Of the first two editions, no known copies exist, and of the 1581 edition there is only a single copy known to exist today.

The appearance, in 1584, of Reginald Scot's *Discoverie of Witchcraft* heralded one of the great dates of conjuring literature. The *Discoverie* contains, among its welter of witchcraft and theology, descriptions and explanations of many of the tricks performed by professional conjurers of that period. (Strictly speaking, a conjurer or conjuror so termed was an evoker of spirits; a conjurer as we know him today being termed a juggler, whilst a juggler, in those days, was called a *tregetour*.)

The *Discoverie of Witchcraft* had as its theme the denial that such a thing as witchcraft existed, which so angered King James the First that he had all available copies burned by the common hangman. As a consequence, the first edition of this book is now very rare. Later editions appeared in 1651, 1654, and 1665, and it was reprinted in 1886 and in 1930.

Practically the whole of the conjuring portion of Scot's work was reissued in 1612, and again in 1614, as *The Art of Jugling* [*sic*] under the "authorship" of one S. R., or Sa. Rid. It was a blatant plagiarism by one whose identity has never been established. (There are some, though, who insist that Sa. Rid. was Samuel Richardson.—W. D.)

In 1634 there appeared another classic of early conjuring literature, which is usually known today as *Hocus Pocus Junior*, although its correct title was *The Anatomie of Legerdemain, by Hocus Pocus Junior*. This ran to some fourteen or so editions, all of which are rare, and served as the model for conjuring books for hundreds of years.

Nearly a century later came H. Dean's *Whole Art of Legerdemain, or Hocus Pocus*, which ran into many editions, and was pirated shamelessly by all and sundry writers on conjuring subjects. In its later editions, its title was reversed to *Hocus Pocus, or the Whole Art of Legerdemain*.

The late eighteenth and early nineteenth centuries saw the advent of many small magical books, some with hand-coloured frontispieces, and these have become great favourites with collectors of magical books.

In the middle of the nineteenth century, conjuring books had reached the stage where the general ambition of the compilers seems to have been the production of a fabulous number of tricks, with the result that the books became padded out with chemical, scientific and arithmetical recreations, the portions devoted to conjuring proper being treated so scantily—and inefficiently—as to be almost useless.

And then a contributor to magazines, a barrister named A. J. Lewis, set out to remedy this state of things. Under the pen-name of "Professor Hoffmann" he wrote, first as a serial in *Every Boy's Magazine*, and then as a book, what has become the world's best-seller in conjuring literature— *Modern Magic*. This work created a furore—especially among magicians!— as it explained the secret of every standard conjuring trick of the day. Hoffmann had a brilliant and facile pen, and was the first to establish the correct principles of teaching conjuring by means of text-books. *Modern Magic* ran into many editions, and was translated into many languages.

Hoffmann (he is hardly ever known by his correct name of Angelo Lewis today) followed his first masterpiece with two other main works, *More Magic* (published in 1890) and *Later Magic* (1904), and a host of minor books and contributions to magazines. Late in his life, when neither health nor financial circumstances were good, he was persuaded, by Harry Houdini, to write *Latest Magic*, which was published in America. This last book, though, shows signs of laboured writing, and the contents are of little worth beside his three great works.

E. T. Sachs, another great writer, published his *Sleight of Hand* in 1877. This finely written book, though, was always overshadowed by the more popular works of Hoffmann.

Another outstanding work was C. Lang Neil's *Modern Conjurer*, first published in 1903. This took Hoffmann's principles of teaching conjuring a step farther by its splendid series of photographs, showing, stage by stage, the actual mechanics of the performance of its tricks.

In 1911 came what was for many years the most serious treatment of the theory of conjuring ever attempted. Written by Nevil Maskelyne and David Devant, *Our Magic* was for a long time read mainly for its remarkable explanations of stage tricks and illusions in the portion written by David Devant. It is only within the last twenty years that the theoretical sections by Nevil Maskelyne have been fully appreciated.

A year later came the first of Will Goldston's locked books (these books were actually fitted with a heavy brass lock and key)—*Exclusive Magical Secrets*. This, although not a well-written work, created as much alarm and consternation among the conjurers as had the earlier *Modern Magic*. Goldston's work contained the methods and secrets of nearly every stage illusion of the period—the heyday of the music-hall. Goldston was shrewd enough to employ clever illustrators for most of his works, with the result that the drawings explained the secrets far better than did the text. He wrote three more large works, *More Exclusive Magical Secrets* (1921), *Further Exclusive Magical Secrets* (1927), and *Great Magicians' Tricks* (1931), besides a host of other books and booklets. He was probably the most prolific conjuring author this country has ever known, but his works are apt to be repetitive.

My Magic Life (1931) and *Secrets of My Magic* (1936), together with *Our Magic*, already mentioned, were the major works of David Devant, one of the world's greatest masters of the magician's art. His smaller works, written in a delightfully simple style, and well illustrated, were most instructive and are today valuable on that account.

The earliest American conjuring book was an edition of H. Dean's *Hocus Pocus*, published in Philadelphia in 1795. This was followed by W. Pinchbeck's *Expositor* (Boston, 1805), Nickerson's *Hocus Pocus* (Baltimore, 1830), the anonymously written *Ventriloquism and Legerdemain Exposed* (Amherst, 1834), Engstrom's *Humorous Magician Unmasked* (Philadelphia, 1836), and many others of the period, all of which are of the greatest rarity.

In 1891, a fraudulent spiritualist medium, who claimed that he had reformed, authored anonymously in St. Paul, Minnesota, *Revelations of a Spirit Medium*. The book exposed the most cherished secrets of fraudulent mediums of the time, and caused such alarm among them that they bought and destroyed every copy they could lay hands on. Under the editorship of the late Harry Price and E. J. Dingwall, a facsimile edition was published in London in 1930.

A great deal of the subject-matter of *Revelations of a Spirit Medium* was used in David P. Abbott's *Behind the Scenes with the Mediums*, published in Chicago in 1907.

A. A. Hopkins' *Magic, Stage Illusions, Etc.*, a large book published in New York in 1897, is full of the most interesting material. It describes the most comprehensive collection imaginable of tricks, illusions, theatrical effects, automata, curious toys, etc.

Also in 1897 was published A. Roterberg's *New Era Card Tricks*, which still remains the finest work on mechanical and trick cards. The book is difficult to obtain, but abridged versions bearing the title *Roterbergs' Card Tricks* are more plentiful.

While on the subject of American books of card tricks, mention must be made of S. W. Erdnase's *Expert at the Card Table*, published in Chicago in 1902. The correct title of the early editions is *Artifice, Ruse and Subterfuge at the*

Card Table. Strictly speaking, this was not a conjuring book, but an instruction manual for card-sharpers, and was described by Professor Hoffmann as being hardly suitable for a Sunday School prize. It did, however, throw an entirely new light on the use of sharpers' sleights for conjuring purposes, and many of the foremost card conjurers of today use methods based on the Erdnase technique.

Scholarly works on the history of conjuring and magic have come from the pen of Dr. Henry Ridgly Evans, at one time a librarian in the Library of Congress, Washington, D.C. His *The Old and the New Magic* (Chicago, 1906) will remain for ever a model of painstaking research and erudition in this field. There was a second edition in 1909, and curiously enough, the second edition is worth considerably more, historically and monetarily, than the first.

Outstanding German works which have been translated into English are Ottokar Fischer's *Hofzinser Kartenkunstler* (Vienna, 1910), translated by S. H. Sharpe as *Hofzinser's Card Tricks*, and Fischer's *Das Wonderbuch der Zauberkunste* (Stuttgart, 1929), translated by J. Barrows Mussey and Fulton J. Oursler as *Illustrated Magic*.

From France came H. Decremps' *Magie Blanche Devoilée* (1784), with its supplemental volumes. The original volume was translated into English by T. Denton, as *The Conjurer Unmasked*.

J. N. Ponsin's *Nouvelle Magie Blanche Devoilée* (Rheims, 1853) was a most painstaking work and was plentifully used by Hoffmann in the formation of *Modern Magic*. The unused portions were translated by S. H. Sharpe in 1937 as *Ponsin on Conjuring*.

J. E. Robert-Houdin, "the father of modern conjuring," wrote a number of interesting books. In 1858 came his *Confidences d'un Prestidigitateur*, translated into English as *The Memoirs of Robert-Houdin*, and still in print. Of his other works may be mentioned *Tricheries des Grecs Devoilée*, *Secrets de la Prestidigitation et de la Magie*, and *Magie et Physique Amusante*. These were translated into English by Hoffmann, as *Card Sharping Exposed*, *Secrets of Conjuring and Magic*, and *Secrets of Stage Conjuring*. *Secrets of Conjuring and Magic* contains the basic principles which are still the foundation stones of conjuring.

What is undoubtedly the finest work ever written, or ever likely to be written, on pure sleight of hand, was published in Paris in 1914 with the title of *Prestidigitation sans Appareils*. Written by Camille Gaultier, a lawyer, it has, within recent years, been translated into English by Jean Hugard, under the title of *Magic without Apparatus*.

Periodicals (on which a separate chapter has been written) form quite a large part of conjuring literature. They may range from a weekly to an annual publication, and their mortality rate is exceptionally high. They fall under three main headings: (1) So-called independent publications (usually dependent upon a magical book publisher); (2) Trade or house organs issued by magical dealers; and (3) Society organs of magical clubs, which are usually circulated to members only.

The first periodical of conjuring interest was *The Conjuror's Magazine*, published monthly in London from 1791 to 1794. It had little relation to conjuring, being more of an astrological publication. Volume 3 was actually titled *The Astrologer's* Magazine.

The first practical conjuring magazine in English was *Mahatma*, published in New York between 1895 and 1906. Other conjuring magazines of note were Stanyon's *Magic* (1900 to 1920), and *The Magician Monthly* (1904 to 1939), both published in London. From America came *The Sphinx* (1902 to 1953), the most popular of all, *Jinx* (1934 to 1941), and *Conjuror's Magazine* (1945 to 1949). The last-named was so lavishly splendid as to be its own undoing.

Today we have in Britain *Abracadabra* (weekly), *The Gen, Wizard, Pentagram, Magical Magazine, Magical Digest* and the leading society's organ *The Magic Circular*, all monthly; *The Magic Wand*, quarterly. In America there are the *New Phoenix* (fortnightly), *Tops, Genii, Hugard's Magic Magazine* and the leading society magazines, *M.U.M.* (Society of American Magicians) and *Linking Ring* (International Brotherhood of Magicians), all monthly.

What of books for the beginner?

There are many of these. Any of the more modern of the books already mentioned will be found useful. The novice will find Hugard's *Modern Magic Manual* and Wilfrid Jonson's *Mr. Smith's Guide to Sleight of Hand* of the greatest value. Paul Clive's *Card Tricks Without Skill* is a real gem of its kind, as well as being a rare bargain at its low price of a few shillings. *The Tarbell Course in Magic*, a monumental work now in its sixth volume, is probably the finest single work of magical instruction to be found anywhere. *Tarbell* is published in America, but is available at seventy shillings a volume from English dealers.

Another first-rate book, but one that assumes the reader to have a certain amount of magical knowledge, is J. N. Hilliard's *Greater Magic*, a most valuable and handsome treatise.

Among the more advanced books are George Kaplan's *Fine Art of Magic*, and Lewis Ganson's *Routined Manipulations* (in three volumes).

Of books dealing with only a single aspect of magic, the following list may be found useful:

Modern Coin Magic, by J. B. Bobo.
Best Tricks with Slates, by Peter Warlock.

The Encyclopedia of Silk Magic, by H. Rice.
The Encyclopedia of Mentalism, by Robert Nelson.
Expert Card Technique, by J. Hugard and F. Braue.
Encyclopedia of Card Tricks, by Jean Hugard.
Encyclopedia of Cigarette Tricks, by Keith Clark.
Encyclopedia of Rope Tricks, by P. Abbott.

Dariel Fitzkee's *Showmanship for Magicians*, *Magic by Misdirection*, and *The Trick Brain* are outstanding works on the methods of presenting conjuring, while for pure theory S. H. Sharpe's *Neo Magic* should be read.

The newcomer to magic will find himself in the midst of a welter of badly duplicated typescript sheets, which, far too often, pass for books on conjuring and sell at high prices. A few of these may be worth the money asked for them, but the majority are of little worth, save, occasionally, to the specialist expert.

One last word of advice to the neophyte seeking conjuring literature: it is of little use asking for conjuring books at one's local bookshop. Most of the worthwhile magical books are sold only—and for good reason!—by magical dealers. But a request for information from these dealers will always bring a prompt response, probably to the effect that the book is already in stock and available.

CHAPTER TWELVE

THE EPHEMERA OF MYSTERY

MAGICIANS have a saying: "If you want to keep a secret, publish it in a magical magazine."

It's an ironical way of suggesting that no conjurer ever pays attention to the hundreds of tricks that are published in magical magazines each year. That's quite wrong, of course, for thousands of magicians buy every copy of the many magazines published for them. What's more, they buy them—most of them—purely to read about the new tricks and how to do them.

The saying may be a cynical implication that the tricks published in magazines won't work. Quite often they won't work, either. Sometimes they work well for one reader, sometimes for all, sometimes, alas, for none. A trick may have worked well for its originator, who was so inspired by it as to put it all down on paper and send it off to one of the magazines. But often, when the reader comes to try it out, something seems to be missing. Maybe it's some flaw in the instructions; perhaps the reader hasn't the ability to perform the trick; maybe the trick is what's known as a pipe-dream, and has never been tried out.

Not many pipe-dreams get into print these days. Competition is keen in the field of magical magazines, and their editors are practical magicians themselves. They watch their material as closely as they watch their circulation figures, and so, for the most part, the tricks that are published in magical periodicals are tricks that will work.

That's not to say that they're always good tricks. But then, the standard of a good trick is such an elusive thing that—well, who are we to say which are good and which aren't?

It's a fact, though, that much excellent material printed in magazines is ignored—until one day a magician startles everyone with a new trick or illusion, and then, most probably, the cry goes up: "Where did he get it? Who invented it? Can I get it?" But the better-informed magicians don't ask such questions. They are more likely to cast a thoughtful eye over their files of magazines, and to ask themselves: "Which one, now?"

Conjurers, you see, are so often lazy people. They will read about a new trick in some magazine, and will lay it aside. "We'll try that out some time," they say, promptly forgetting all about it. And then, months or years later, they are reminded of that trick they thought they'd think about—by seeing another magician perform it. It's been left to some more enterprising reader to find the hidden touchstone that converted dry-as-dust reading into a miracle. That's the way it is, and that's the way, no doubt, it always will be.

Yes, the magical magazines have produced some miracles over the years. Have you ever seen a magician put his lady assistant's neck beneath the blade of a "guillotine" and then crash down the blade, which passes through her neck without injuring it? You have? That illusion first appeared in a magazine.

You must have seen, too, the conjurer who shows you an empty tube, about a foot long, from which he extracts dozens upon dozens of yards of colourful silk. That's known as the Ghost Tube, and it's used today by thousands of conjurers. The Ghost Tube, too, appeared as a trick in a magazine.

You may remember, too, Brian MacCarthy, in one of the Magic Circle's television broadcasts, pushing two candles into a slim metal tube just big enough to hold one candle, and then taking them out again and proving that they *weren't* telescopic, or hollow, but just two ordinary candles, and that the tube was nothing more than a tight-fitting brass tube. That's another magazine item. It must have been passed over by everyone who read it, years ago, until they saw it actually performed, with great success, by its inventor.

These three tricks—picked at random from hundreds of others—appeared in the world's oldest surviving magazine for conjurers, *The Magic Wand*.

There were magazines for magicians half a century and more before *The Magic Wand* was first published, but none of them is with us today.

Let's go back fifty years or so to the year 1905, to No. 4 Duke Street, off London's Strand. Over the doorway was the sign, "Ornum's Magical Depository. G. M. Ornum, the Wizard of the East." Inside, you could buy anything magical, from a cushion that howled like a startled cat when sat upon, to a large and imposing metal canister that contained an ingenious mechanism to substitute an undamaged handkerchief for one that had just been burnt. The audiences of that leisurely day loved these mechanical miracles, and Ornum always had a good stock of them.

The proprietor of Ornum's, Mr. George M. Munro, decided to publish a magazine for conjurers, to be called *The Wizard*, and to appear monthly. As editor of his magazine he employed P. T. Selbit (*his* real name was

Tibbles), one of the greatest inventive geniuses in magic, and the man who invented the illusion known as Sawing a Woman in Half.

The first number of *The Wizard* appeared in September 1905, and was filled with theatrical gossip, new tricks and sound theory. After seeing the magazine firmly established, Selbit left the editor's chair, and Ornum took his place. Selbit was a busy man, running a vaudeville act under several different names, and had little time to sit down in Duke Street and edit a magazine, much as he loved the job.

Ornum changed the name of his magazine to *The Magic Wand*, and it continued in the same style and format for three and a half years, when it was taken over by Mr. George Johnson. At the end of Volume 7, Mr. Johnson joined the Forces, for we were in the middle of World War I, and the magazine suspended publication until the editor returned from service.

In 1921, George Johnson went over to quarterly publication, and moved his office to 24 Buckingham Street, Strand. Many were the famous magicians who called there to pass the time of day. The office was a recognised rendezvous for magicians from all over the world, and each one was invited to take a seat in the editor's old bentwood chair. When Mr. Johnson retired from *The Magic Wand* in later years, he presented the old chair to the Magic Circle, and today it stands in the Circle's museum. There's nothing special about it, but it's just one of those ordinary things that has acquired a long tradition through its association with the great magicians of the past.

During the next twenty-four years, *The Wand* appeared regularly each quarter, and its pages contained many of the tricks and illusions that are today regarded as classics of the magic art. Right through the second world war, George Johnson never missed publishing an issue each quarter, although often, when he came to the office in the morning, he would see new and fearful damage to buildings in the vicinity, where enemy bombs had blasted the region of Charing Cross Station overnight.

In 1945, when George Johnson was thinking of retiring, young George Armstrong, a London magician, had just been demobilised after six years in the Royal Artillery. The two of them came to terms, and Armstrong took over *The Magic Wand* and continued to publish it quarterly.

In 1947 Armstrong revived the name of the old *Wizard* as a monthly magazine, and this continues publication today as a popular "slick" style of magic magazine.

In 1953 George Armstrong set the magical world a-chatter by changing the whole style of *The Magic Wand*, increasing its page size, adding additional pages, commissioning more and more illustrations by Jack Lamonte (a well-known magician who combines all the qualities of a first-rate artist with his talent for magic) and seeking the best writing brains throughout the

English-speaking world. Bound together in one annual volume, *The Wand* contains something like 200 original tricks, ranging from impromptu tricks with matches, coins, or playing cards, to stage and platform tricks and full-scale illusions.

If I were asked to pick out the best trick from the fifty-year file of *The Magic Wand*, I think I'd select the one in which the magician pours the contents of a quart jug of beer into a pint glass, without a drop overflowing. He then pours the whole pint into a half-pint glass—and still nothing over-flows. Then the half-pint is poured into a smaller glass, and from that into a whisky tot, and still nothing has flowed over the top of a single glass. The magician holds up the glasses one at a time as he pours out the liquid, and he finally vanishes the last little drop by drinking it. The idea of this baffling trick was thought out by a professional magician, Benson Dulay, and the method of making it work by George Armstrong.

As well as *The Magic Wand* and *The Wizard*, the enterprising Armstrong publishes a third magical periodical, *The Pentagram*. This monthly magazine of eight pages an issue caters for the specialist and the advanced student of magic. *The Pentagram* was started in October, 1946, by a Nottingham bank official who is also a member of the Inner Magic Circle, and who is known in the magical world as Peter Warlock. In 1948, Warlock's business commitments took him to Wallington, Surrey, and the following year pressure of business compelled him to entrust George Armstrong with publication of his *Pentagram*.

Warlock continues to edit *The Pentagram*, however, and contributes many of his own extremely subtle effects to its pages. The bulk of the magazine's contents have always consisted of high-quality mental magic and simple direct effects with everyday objects. But simple in effect though they may be, they frequently call for a high degree of manipulative ability and performing skill.

Peter Warlock is one of the most knowledgeable fellows in magic, besides being—when he chooses—one of the most aggressive. At the drop of a hat he will enter a controversy, often to the dismay of the other participants, but always to the delight of the onlookers. A man who usually knows exactly what he's talking about, Warlock isn't to be put down by fallacious argument or by weight of numbers.

Let's turn from Peter Warlock to another man who loves an argument. And to conjure him up, there's no more appropriate spell than the ancient incantation . . . ABRACADABRA!

When the man in the street hears that word he at once thinks of magic. But to the magician, it means the name of a magazine—the world's only weekly periodical devoted to the art. For the past ten years, wizards throughout the English-speaking world (and many a foreigner, too) have bought this weekly quota of magical news, reviews, tricks and chit-chat.

There are, and have been for many years, monthly and quarterly magazines for the magician, but the long wait between issues, and the problem of distance—there are, for example, very many active performers as far away as Australia and New Zealand—make a weekly publication almost essential. It provides a regular and unfailing link to bind together the conjuring fraternity. Until Goodliffe, publisher and editor-in-chief of *Abracadabra*, launched his magazine, there had been no lasting link. Previous attempts to publish a magical weekly had been made in 1910 and in 1926, but they were at that time aiming at much too small a market, and so died a speedy, if lamented, death. Since then, the numbers of people interested in magic have increased incredibly swiftly, and although even now 2,000 copies an issue seems small, compared with the big-circulation popular magazines, it is a formidable number when one considers that this little weekly is sold only to magicians.

Abracadabra is, to the conjurer, much more than just a magazine. Since it was inaugurated, magical gatherings have been held under its auspices, attracting hundreds of wizards to Birmingham, the city of its origin. Well-known performers have been brought over from America and the Continent to appear in shows arranged specially for magicians. The editor has travelled to more than a dozen different countries to report magical conventions. The little band of hand-picked magicians whom he takes with him on some of these overseas trips have even founded their own "Flying Sorcerers". Club— surely the most exclusive organisation of magicians in the world.

One outstanding example of Goodliffe's enterprise came when the Magic Circle Golden Jubilee celebrations were held in London in April 1955. Goodliffe opened temporary editorial offices in the building where the celebrations were held and published a *daily* edition of *Abracadabra*. This unique journalistic venture not only provided day-to-day news of the Magic Circle's great celebrations, but also became at once an historic record of events and a series of collector's pieces to be snapped up before they were sold out.

Goodliffe and his staff are particularly proud of the success of their magical weekly, because America—which country is reported to have more magicians and near-magicians than any other in the world—is traditionally the home of the go-ahead businessman; yet in this sphere it was left to Britain to lead the world. *Abracadabra* is, therefore, not only a considerable factor in upholding British prestige, but is also a satisfactory dollar-earner for the Government.

In the autumn of 1955, *Abra* (as the magazine is universally known among magicians) published its 500th issue, coinciding with its 500th consecutive week of appearing dead on time. It is, in fact, the only British weekly to achieve this record, for all other weeklies were suspended for two weeks during the fuel crisis of 1947. That fuel crisis caused a few headaches in the *Abra* office, too, but the magazine appeared, nevertheless, by some private magic known only to Goodliffe and Fabian, his right-hand man.

There have been lots of high-spots in this 500-week achievement. The editor's first visit to America, for instance, had something of the flavour of a triumphal progress, covering 12,000 miles in eighteen days, by way of New Orleans, Atlantic City, Chicago, Detroit and New York. Then there was his visit to the Isle of Man, where he was asked to entertain the Governor; to Paris, where he received a French Government decoration for his services to the art of magic; and to Barcelona, where he saw much magic—and a bullfight.

Goodliffe's only regret, he says, is that he is a columnist whose field is strictly limited to magical matters, but he hints darkly that the stories he *could* tell of related experiences in other directions would fill a book or two.

Goodliffe, by the way, is never referred to as "Mr. Goodliffe," or even by the prefacing of a Christian name or initial. He is always just Goodliffe. Few magicians know the reason, but the explanation is a simple one. Goodliffe is his Christian name. Under his surname, he is a well-known Birmingham businessman, as well as being a prominent figure in the world of religion.

Like Peter Warlock, Goodliffe is a tough customer when it comes to an argument, and does not hesitate to express his often controversial—and sometimes, let us whisper, misguided—theories in the pages of his magazine.

But in person, you couldn't wish for a more genial, inoffensive citizen. His outstanding features are—and he would be the last to take exception to the fact going on record—his ears. A small, compactly built fellow, Goodliffe is blessed with a pair of ears that can best be described as of handsome construction.

At one gathering of magicians, the committee, of which Goodliffe was a member, solemnly filed on to the platform wearing enormous false ears. Goodliffe was wearing the ears Nature gave him. The committee members—Goodliffe included—maintained perfectly straight faces, although the audience were in stitches of laughter.

Came the time for Goodliffe to speak. His opening remarks were: "I dare say you think I have big ears, but I'll let you into a secret. These aren't my real ears I'm wearing. I carry my own ears in my pocket."

And from his pocket he carefully drew out a pair of false ears far, far bigger than those worn by the other committeemen. By then Goodliffe was the only person in that large hall who could keep a straight face.

It seems hard to imagine what the magical scene was like before this elfish character brightened things up with *Abra*—and the Goodliffe ears. It's even harder to imagine what conjurers would do without their weekly *Abra*, which is a highly efficient specialist weekly newspaper reporting an incredibly wide range of magical activities from all over the world.

A monthly magazine for magicians which has built up great prestige and an impressive circulation since the war is Harry Stanley's *Gen*. Its first issues were being published as a modest leaflet before its proprietor was demobilised at the end of the war. When Harry left the Services and returned to his business as a magical dealer, the magazine fairly leapt to the fore.

For some years now its principal articles have been written by Lieut.-Col. Lewis Ganson, a prolific writer on magical subjects, and also a first-class practical magician and an expert on the theory of magic. Ganson has the ability of developing a well-known trick, by simple, easy methods, until it becomes a master mystery. He also has the much rarer ability of being able to write about it so that his readers can at once understand the methods of working, and with only a very little practice can perform the trick creditably. Add to this the wonderful photographic illustrations he provides, and you have the perfect lessons in magic.

Ganson's three-volume work on *Routined Manipulation* consists largely of his articles in *The Gen*, and is invaluable to the student and the expert alike.

The Magic Magazine, published by Max Andrews, the magical dealer who was formerly manager of Hamley's conjuring department, is also a monthly, and can always be relied to provide excellent material. Prominent among its contributors is Eddie Joseph, a highly skilled expert on sleight of hand and misdirection, who recently came to London from India, where he had created a world-wide reputation for his writings.

Oscar Oswald, another magical dealer, publishes *The Magical Digest*, which includes unusual articles on many subjects allied to conjuring, such as Punch and Judy, puppetry, ventriloquism and the like.

One of the most remarkable and valuable magical magazines is in the form of a newspaper, published quarterly by Jack Hughes, of Colindale, London. This is *Hughes' News*, and although it is a newcomer, comparatively speaking, in the field of magical journalism, it has a wide following. Hughes is noted throughout the world for the fine quality of his woodwork in the production of magical apparatus, and his *Hughes' News* comes well up to the standard of his other work.

Eight magical magazines in Britain alone—one weekly, five monthlies, and two quarterlies—may seem a large number, considering that magic is pretty well a closed shop. But each one has its large circle of devoted readers, and although you'll never see any of these magazines on your newsagent's bookstall, each has a wide circulation.

There are others, too, which I haven't mentioned. Most of the magical societies publish a bulletin, ranging from the modest duplicated sheet once every few months to the handsome, glossy *Magic Circular*, official organ of the Magic Circle, and only available to members. Mr. John Young, editor of the *Magic Circular*, is the borough engineer in a London borough, and he calculates that the production of the magazine takes up just about as much time in his leisure hours as he spends in his council offices on his own profession.

The British Ring of the International Brotherhood of Magicians has its own *Budget*, and the London Society of Magicians publishes its *Gazette*, but again these are for members only, and the magician outside these organisations is seldom likely to see either of them.

In other countries, the spate of magical literature is perhaps not so voluminous as in Britain, although the U.S.A. runs us pretty close. For fifty years the magical scene in America was dominated by a fine monthly magazine, *The Sphinx*, edited in its latter years by John Mulholland, a scholarly writer and a splendid performer and lecturer. Then, quite suddenly, *The Sphinx* ceased publication, to everyone's lasting regret. During its fifty years it had attracted to its pages articles by every great magician of the half-century, besides creating many up-and-coming young writers whose names are now internationally known. A complete file of *The Sphinx* today is almost beyond value.

Another magazine that came to a sudden end in the U.S.A. was *The Jinx*, a small weekly—though it had started its career as a monthly— published, edited, typed, and often written throughout by a magician named Theodore Annemann. *The Jinx*, too, is priceless today, and the tricks it published are in many cases household words among magicians. Annemann, its founder, was an odd character, with an eye for the sensational. His own particular line of magic was thought-reading, and his skill in this branch of the art was legendary in his own lifetime. But nobody felt that they really knew Annemann the man. Married twice, he indulged such foibles as keeping tame bats in his New York apartment, and fixing mirrors outside the windows of rooms so that each room overlooked the next.

His magazine might have been running today, but one night when his wife returned to their apartment she found the doors locked. When they were opened, she found Theodore Annemann lying, full length on the floor, with a rubber mask over his face, connected to a gaspipe.

Annemann died on the eve of what could have been his greatest show. He had booked a New York theatre to perform therein the trick that has been so unlucky for countless magicians—Catching the Bullets. He was to have had a rifle fired at him, and would have caught the bullets in his mouth, as he had done often enough before when performing outdoors.

Jinx Number 151 was the last issue of his magazine. Try to buy a complete set today, and you will find that you need many pounds to acquire it.

Today's magical periodicals in U.S.A. include three of importance— Jean Hugard's *Magic Monthly*, Jay Marshall's *Phoenix*, and Geraldine Larsen's *Genii and Conjuror's Magazine*.

Jean Hugard, now in his eighties and almost completely blind and deaf, is the world's Grand Old Man of Magic. An Australian who now lives in Brooklyn, New York, he was for many years a vaudeville illusionist who had shown at all the world's great theatres. Many of his miracles have never since been repeated, for Hugard is the only man who holds the key to them.

He started his *Hugard's Magic Monthly* in 1944, and has never missed a month since. In the twelve years *Hugard's* has been running it has increased its size to a 12-page or 16-page publication, and many, many fine tricks have been explained therein. But of even greater value than the tricks is the advice Hugard gives to his readers. Sometimes he will write a full-page article on magical presentation. Sometimes he will drop a single line in to fill up a column. But that single line contains the essence of the wisdom of Hugard's long life and experience.

Many thinking magicians place *Hugard's* at the top of the list of magical periodicals, a place it richly merits.

When Annemann's *Jinx* closed down on the death of its publisher, an American novelist and short-story writer, Bruce Elliott, stepped into the field as a publisher and established a similar periodical, designed to replace *The Jinx*. That was *The Phoenix*, which is still running strongly today, and looks like going on for ever. Elliott found that his story-writing commitments were too heavy to allow him to continue the magazine (he has a phenomenal output of stories for the United States Press) and he handed it over to Jay Marshall, that polished performer who scored such a success at London's Palladium—Mecca of every vaudeville artiste in the world—in 1955.

The Genii was started before the war by a Los Angeles lawyer named Bill Larsen. Magic, though, held prime place in his affections, and it was as a magician and editor, rather than as a lawyer, that we always remember him. A few years ago he bought up a large, handsome, colourful—but poorly edited—magazine called *Conjuror's Magazine*, which he amalgamated with his own *Genii*.

The Genii has attracted some clever writers and magicians to its pages, notable among whom is Dariel Fitzkee, who does the book reviews. Fitzkee is an acoustics engineer in California, but from time to time he plays truant and takes a magic show out on the road, touring the United States and the American republics.

Bill Larsen died not many years ago, and his widow, Geraldine, took over the magazine. Gerrie Larsen is not only a good magazine editor, but is also an established magician of high repute, with a big following on television in America. Her *Genii* is a bright magazine, carrying dealers' advertisements from all over the world. If you want to buy a special breed of miniature, pink-eyed rabbits to produce from your top hat, you'll find them advertised in *Genii*. If you want to know what the magical dealers of the world have to sell to you, *Genii's* advertising columns will tell you.

I am not including here what I consider to be the biggest magical magazine of them all—*The Linking Ring*. This is the official organ of the International Brotherhood of Magicians, and I had something to say about it in the chapter devoted to that organisation.

So much for current magazines. What of the past? The subject is so complex, and the field so wide, that whole books could be written about magical magazines of the past. There have been, for hundreds of years, astrological publications, but the practical conjurer usually has little time for these.

Until 1895 there was little or nothing in the way of magical journalism, but in that year George H. Little, of New York, founded *Mahatma*. It ran erratically for about ten years, and by today's standards was somewhat crudely produced, but its literary content was of a very high standard.

In England, Ellis Stanyon, of Hampstead, was a prominent magical writer for many years. His *Stanyon's Magic*, in periodical numbers, is a rare item indeed today among the magical bibliophiles.

Will Goldston, of London, a magical dealer with a reputedly haunted studio off Leicester Square, edited various magazines in his time, ranging from Gamage's publication, *The Magician*, when he managed their conjuring department, to a series of card index entries describing sundry tricks.

Harry Houdini, that brash, bouncing, publicity-conscious hero of the handcuffs, himself edited a magazine for magicians early in the century. For two years he ran *The Conjurors' Magazine* (the title taken from an ancient astrological publication, and later adopted by the periodical taken over by Larsen) from New York. Then, quite suddenly, and without a whisper of warning, he dropped it. A pity, for it was, in format and content alike, one of the most attractive ever produced. Good type, excellent paper, skilful make-up and printing, set it apart in the world of magical journalism.

Possibly the oddest of all the magical magazines come from India. To read some of these is sufficient to disillusion one sadly on the subject of the "mysterious East." Some of the Indian magazines print the most extraordinary stuff. The simplest and easiest of Western tricks are glorified as miracles of perfection. Many of these phenomenal mysteries have been appearing year after year in the Christmas numbers of English magazines, in those sections devoted to simple party tricks for the young, or in books of tricks published for schoolboys. But the Indian magician apparently relishes them. Maybe he has reason to do so, for they are at least practical, which is more than one can say of the Indian Rope Trick.

There are times, however, when the Indian magazine editor lapses into the esoteric, and you may find among the apparatus needed to perform some item such oddments as the blood of a cobra, the skull of a monkey, and the like.

But the purpose of this chapter is not to review the history of magical literature of the past, nor to comment upon that of the present. Its purpose is, rather, to provide some information for the present reader on what is available to him in the way of conjuring periodicals. Experience shows that nine out of ten magicians owe their first interest in practical magic to something they read, rather than someone they saw. Often, that something read was a magical magazine, and reading it provided the spark of interest that spread to a flame of fascination. Sometimes, mind you, the spark was effectively smothered by the wet blanket of criticism in the family circle (for the members of one's family are devastating critics of one's early prowess as a magician).

But that's another story altogether. . . .

GLOSSARY OF CONJURING TERMS

Acquitment: Series of moves involved in a sleight, usually to make something vanish, or to keep it hidden.

Act: The complete rehearsed programme as presented.

Assembly: A card trick in which several cards of a kind are brought together, e.g. the four aces, or all the cards of a suit.

Backpalm: To conceal an object at the back of the hand.

Bight: A loop of rope, string, etc., contained in a knot.

Bill tube: A sealed tube in which a bank note is made to appear.

Billet: Small slip of paper on which something is written or drawn.

Biseauté: Adjective applied to cards that are narrower at one end than the other. (See *Stripper*.)

Black-art Principle: The principle that black upon black shows no join, or that black upon black is invisible when bright lights are directed towards the audience.

Black light: Fluorescent lighting, invisible until it falls upon specially treated surfaces. By its use, treated objects are seen, even though in complete darkness.

Blind Shuffle: A shuffle which retains the cards in their original order. (See *False Shuffle*.)

Bottom card: The card on the face of pack; the card whose face can be seen when the pack is assembled.

Bottom deal: The dealing of the bottom card of the pack, secretly, instead of the top card.

Bottom stock: That portion of a pack of cards which is at the bottom.

Box: To cause cards to face each other in the pack.

Brainwave deck: A specially prepared pack of cards which can be used to show any card as reversed in the pack.

Break: A small gap held in some particular place in a pack of cards, and maintained by (usually) the tip of a finger.

Breakaway wand: A magic wand which wilts and breaks up when held by a spectator.

Bridge: A gap in the pack of cards, caused by bending some cards.

Card box: A box for vanishing, exchanging, or producing a playing card. The Roterberg Card Box is the standard piece of this equipment.

Charlier system: A system of marking cards, originally by pricking minute holes in them at specified places. Named after its originator, who was a nineteenth-century conjurer and magical inventor.

Conjurer's choice: No choice! (See *Force.*)

Crimp: To bend one corner of a card secretly.

Cull: To extract, or assemble together secretly, a number of cards.

Cut: To divide the pack into two or more sections openly. *A complete cut* is made when the portions are reassembled.

Daub: A paste for marking cards on the backs or faces.

Deck: American (and old English) term for a pack of cards.

Diachylon: A chemical substance used for making two cards adhere together.

Ditch: Slang term, often used in magic, meaning "To get rid of something."

Double-backer: Special cards, printed with a back on each side.

Double-facer: Ditto, but printed with a face on each side.

Double lift: To lift two cards as one.

Dovetail: To shuffle cards by interlacing them.

Drape: The overhang of a table cover or table-cloth.

Drop: To drop the balance of cards held in the hand during a shuffle, so that they fall upon the shuffled cards.

Effect: Description of a trick as seen by the audience.

End-grip: To hold a pack of cards with the thumb at one end and fingers at the other.

Erdnase: Pen-name of a writer (S. W. Erdnase) who claimed to be a reformed gambler, and who wrote a book called *Artifice, Ruse and Subterfuge at the Card Table* (usually known as *The Expert at the Card Table*) which exposed gamblers' sleights with cards. Legend has it that S. W. Erdnase's real name was E. S. Andrews.

Face card: See *Bottom card.*

Fair shuffle: A genuine shuffle of the cards, as against a false shuffle.

Fake: *Not* "Feke." A fake is a piece of apparatus, seemingly unprepared, which has been secretly prepared for the purpose of the trick. Frequently the presence of the apparatus itself is unsuspected by the audience.

False count: To count cards, coins, etc., so as to show them as totalling more or less than their real number.

False cut: To appear to cut the pack of cards, while really leaving it in its previous order.

False shuffle: To shuffle the cards without changing their order.

Fan: To manipulate playing cards into the form of a fan.

First card: The top card of the pack when the pack is held face down. Or the first card to be dealt, whether face up or face down.

Flash paper: Tissue paper treated with explosive chemicals so that it ignites with a brilliant flash when touched with anything hot.

Flash wand: A magic wand which emits a bright flash of fire when the control is operated.

Force: To restrict a spectator's choice to one item.

French drop: See *Tourniquet.*

Ghost tube: A tube which can be shown apparently empty, while holding goods to be produced later.

Gimmick: A secret piece of apparatus which is largely responsible for the success of a trick.

Glide: To hold back a card and deal the next card to it from under the pack.

Glimpse: Secretly to catch sight of a card, a piece of writing, or something else which is supposed to be concealed from the performer.

Grandmother's necklace: An old principle of threading beads so that they can be un-threaded instantly, on which many modern rope, string and tape tricks are based.

Hindu shuffle: A method of shuffling cards in which the pack is held on the long sides by each hand, one hand drawing out a batch of cards and replacing them elsewhere. Not practised among card players in Britain.

Holdout: A secret device for containing articles—usually playing cards—so that they are hidden and yet at the disposal of the operator when needed. A holdout sometimes extracts the cards from the pack and retains them until wanted.

Homing: The magical return of an object, e.g. a card, coin, ball, etc., to its original place after it has been removed therefrom.

Indifferent card: A card other than that with which the trick is being performed. Any card not being used.

Injog: To replace a card on the pack so that its end projects towards the operator.

Jog: To replace a card with its end projecting slightly.

Key card: A card which is distinctive in some way, so that it can readily be identified by the magician. (See *Locator.*)

Knife force: To force a card on a spectator by means of a knife thrust into the pack.

Levitation: The raising of an object or a person into the air without any visible means of support. (See also *Suspension.*)

Load: An article or collection of articles prepared so that it can be secretly inserted into a container for production later.

Locator: A card, specially prepared in some secret way, which can be used for locating other cards. (See also *Key card.*)

Long card: A playing card which is slightly longer than the rest of the pack. Also, a joke card which is several times longer than a normal card, and on which the pips are printed in a long line.

Masking principle:	To cover secretly an article with something that matches its surface exactly.
Mechanic's grip:	The card-sharper's way of holding cards when dealing. This term is seldom used in Britain.
Mene tekel pack:	A pack of cards made up of twenty-six cards, each card being duplicated once.
Mentalism:	The branch of conjuring usually known as thought-reading, mindreading, clairvoyance, etc.
Misdirection:	The art of misleading the spectator's attention at the critical moment, e.g. to flourish an empty hand in which an article is supposed to be concealed, while secretly disposing of the article with the other hand.
Mockers:	A brand of marked playing cards sold in Britain. Not recommended for conjuring purposes, as their secret is known to many laymen and schoolboys.
Move:	The manipulation required to perform a trick.
Nail nick:	To mark an object secretly by pressing with the thumb or finger nail.
Nikola system:	A valuable system of memory training applied to conjuring, originated by Louis Nikola, a famous magician and magical inventor. It is based upon association of ideas.
Okito box:	A box used in coin conjuring, in which the secret preparation is absolutely imperceptible. Invented by the famous American magician, Okito (Theo. Bamberg).
One-way pack:	A pack of cards with an asymmetrical design on the backs.
Outjog:	To replace a card on the pack so that its edge projects away from the operator.
Overhand shuffle:	The normal way of shuffling cards in Britain, in which the cards, held edgewise in the left hand, are picked up and replaced in batches by the right hand.
Pack:	A pack of cards. In Great Britain and America the usual number is fifty-two, with one or two jokers and sometimes a blank card. On the Continent many packs number only thirty-two cards.
Palm:	To conceal a small article in the hand secretly.
Pass:	A pass used to be the description of a gesture which accompanied a "magic word." Nowadays it usually signifies the secret exchanging of position of two halves of a pack of cards (or two similar objects). In America this is sometimes known as "Jumping the Cut."
Pass off:	To convey away, secretly, some article which is carried offstage by an assistant or a mechanical device.
Peek:	To sight a card or other object quickly and secretly.
Prearrangement:	The arrangement, beforehand, of articles (e.g. a pack of cards) in some recognised order.

Principle: Method by which a particular kind of trick, or series of tricks, is performed.

Production: The production of articles from a container that has previously been shown empty, or from "thin air." In some illusions, living people are so produced.

Prop: Short for "Property"—the apparatus, seen and unseen, required for the performance of a trick. Also, such items as conjurers' tables, stands, and utility items are "props."

Pull: A secret device of mechanical construction for removing an article secretly from one place to another. The pull could be a simple piece of elastic to make a ring disappear up the sleeve, or it could be as complicated as that required to move a heavy object completely off the stage.

Readers: Playing cards marked on the backs so that the magician can "read" their values without seeing their faces. Not as frequently used as the public suspect.

Recovery: The resumption of control of an article used in magic, e.g. the regaining of a billiard ball secretly placed under the arm and hidden.

Reset: To prepare afresh a piece of apparatus which required such preparation, e.g. to wind up a secret piece of clockwork before performance, or to adjust a secret trapdoor so that it is ready for use.

Reversed card: A playing card which is returned to the pack either back to front or upside down.

Ribbon spread: To lay out the cards in a long line by a single sweep of the hand.

Riffle: To thumb the ends of the cards so that one card falls rapidly after another. The *Riffle shuffle* is performed in this manner. (See *Dovetail.*)

Rope cement: A chemical substance sometimes used for joining two pieces of rope.

Roughing fluid: A chemical fluid which, when applied to playing cards, roughens their surface. Can be made at home by the mixture of Canada balsam and carbon-tetrachloride.

Routine: The showmanlike arrangement of a trick or series of tricks so that they blend naturally and most effectively.

Run: To slide off one card at a time when shuffling a pack of cards.

Second deal: To deal the second card from the top of the pack instead of the first card. This requires great skill and constant practice to perform adequately, and few magicians can second deal imperceptibly. Nearly always, the manner of holding the cards in the left hand gives away the secret to the spectator.

Set (to):   To prepare a piece of apparatus ready for the conjurer's performance. (See also *Reset.*)

Set-up: The prearrangement of apparatus, almost always playing cards, which are arranged in a certain order.

Servante: A hidden shelf or suspended pocket, usually behind the table or chair, or else concealed by some other piece of apparatus.

Shift: Another name for the *Pass* with cards.

Short card: A playing card which is shorter than the rest of the pack.

Shuffle: To mix playing cards.

Shuffle off: To conclude a false shuffle by genuinely shuffling the balance of the pack.

Side-grip: To hold a pack of cards by its long edges.

Sight: See *Glimpse* and *Peek.*

Sleeve (to): To insert secretly an article in the sleeve. This principle is not used nearly as often as popular belief would have it, but when it *is* used the skilled conjurer makes it completely imperceptible and deceiving. A good sleeve-worker has the uncanny skill of a juggler and the precision of a marksman.

Sleight: The secret manipulation required to perform a trick, often calling for a high degree of digital dexterity combined with sense of balance and timing.

Slick card: A card which is highly polished so that it slides more easily than the rest of the pack.

Slip: A card sleight, in which the top card of the pack is imperceptibly placed on the lower half of the pack when the cards are cut.

Square: To adjust the edges of playing cards by pressing them into alignment with the fingers and thumb after the cards have, say, been shuffled.

Stack: A prearranged pack of cards.

Stage money: Imitation money, usually in bank notes, that is used for stage purposes, including conjuring. Good imitations of genuine notes are rare, as it is illegal to make or possess such items.

Steal: To abstract an article secretly, e.g. to palm a card from the pack while handing it to be shuffled.

Steamboats: A particular kind of playing card with a plaid design on the backs, particularly favoured by card manipulators because of their smoothness and flexibility. Also, "Steamboat" is the description applied to cards having no white border on the backs.

Stock: The main portion of a pack of cards, as against those cards being immediately dealt or otherwise used for playing or magical purposes. Sometimes called the *Talon.*

Stooge: A secret confederate in the audience.

Strippers: Playing cards that are wider at one end than the other. (See *Biseauté.*)

Switch: To exchange one article for another, usually secretly.

Suspension:	To *maintain* an object or person in mid-air without apparent support, as against *Levitation*, which is to *raise and lower* an object or a person.
Tabled card:	The card on the table, as against those in the hand.
Talking:	Noise made by apparatus when in use—always undesirable and a source of worry to the magician afflicted with talking apparatus. E.g. a secret spring when released emits a loud clank, thus betraying the presence of some mechanism.
Tarot:	Cards, longer and narrower than playing cards, and seventy-eight in number, used in fortune-telling and for some card games in Central France. The symbols on the faces have occult and esoteric significance, and are of great interest to the student. A set of Tarot cards is known as a "book," rather than a pack. Not recommended for conjuring purposes, as some of the cards have religious significance to some people.
Throw:	To deposit the balance of cards on the rest after a shuffle.
Thumb-count:	The art of secretly counting cards held in the hand by the thumb—a specialised sleight calling for great skill.
Top card:	The card lying face down on top of the pack.
Top stock:	The upper section of the pack of cards when the pack is held face downwards.
Tourniquet:	The act of pretending to take an object in one hand while really leaving it in the other. Also called the *French drop*.
Transposition:	The exchange of position between one object and another. E.g. a bottle is placed under the right-hand tube of two tubes and is later found under the left-hand tube, the right-hand tube being shown empty.
Undercut:	To take the lower section of a pack of cards and place it on the upper section.
Uppercut:	To take the upper section and place it beneath the lower section of the pack.
Vanish:	Used as a verb in magic, and meaning to make an article disappear.
Wax:	Conjurers' wax is a variety of bee's-wax obtainable in various colours for causing cards, coins and other articles to adhere to each other or to something else.
Well:	A secret cavity, usually in the conjurer's table, and concealed by the *Black-art principle*.
Woofle dust:	An imaginary powder used by conjurers who require an excuse to put a hand in a pocket "to get the woofle dust." Its use usually signifies a lack of imagination or digital skill.
Zinc stearate:	A chemical powder used for making cards smooth and easily manipulated.

CLASSIFIED LIST OF MAGICAL SOCIETIES*

Aberdeen: ABERDEEN MAGICAL SOCIETY
Secretary: Ian Williams, 5 Marine Place, Aberdeen.
Headquarters: Imperial Hotel, Aberdeen.
Meetings: alternate Tuesdays, 8 p.m.

Ayr: AYR BROTHER CONJURERS
Sec.: Robert Caldwell, 35 Sandgate, Ayr, Scotland.

Barnsley: BARNSLEY CIRCLE OF MAGICIANS
Sec.: Horace Cooper, 55 Shaw Lane, Barnsley.
H.Q.: Three Cranes Hotel, Eldon Street, Barnsley.
Meetings: alternate Fridays, 7.45 p.m.

Bath: BATH CIRCLE OF MAGICIANS
Sec.: A. Harper, Ridgeway, Kingsdown, Box, Wilts.
H.Q.: Oldfield Boys' School, Bath.
Meetings: every Friday.

Belfast: ULSTER SOCIETY OF MAGICIANS
Sec.: Ted Oldham, 26 Summerhill Park, Belfast.
H.Q.: Kensington Hotel.
Meetings: first Monday of month.

Birkenhead: WIRRAL MAGICAL SOCIETY
Sec.: Robert Foster, 45 Bankville Road, Tranmere, Birkenhead.

Birmingham: BRITISH MAGICAL SOCIETY
Sec.: Eric Hampton, 47 Halesowen Road, Birmingham 32.
H.Q.: 79 Edmund Street, Birmingham.
Meetings: 2nd, 3rd and 4th Tuesdays, 7 p.m.
STAFFORDSHIRE MAGICAL SOCIETY
Sec.: Norman H. Parry, 62 Merrivale Road, Smethwick, Staffs.
H.Q.: Toc H Hall, City Road, Edgbaston, Birmingham.
Meetings: alternate Sundays, 3 p.m.

Blackburn: MODERN MYSTIC LEAGUE
Sec.: A. Strack, 226 Brownhill Drive, Blackburn.
H.Q.: K. S. C. Clubrooms, Cort Street, Blackburn.
Meetings: 2nd Sunday each month, 2 p.m.

* Reproduced from *The Magician's Diary and Year Book, 1956,* by kind permission of the publishers, The Penshaw Press, 59 Hunts Mead, Billericay, Essex.

Blackpool:	BLACKPOOL MAGIC CIRCLE
	Sec.: C. H. Fitness, 1a Ribble Road, Central Drive, Blackpool.
	Meetings: 2nd and 4th Thursdays.
Bournemouth:	WESSEX MAGICAL ASSOCIATION
	Sec.: Mrs. W. Laurie, 6 Marlborough Road, Bournemouth.
	H.Q.: Grand Hotel, Bournemouth.
	Meetings: 2nd Tuesday each month, 7.30 p.m.
Bradford:	BRADFORD MAGIC CIRCLE
	Sec.: Ken Tordoff, 175 Otley Road, Bradford 3.
	H.Q.: Alexander Hotel, Great Horton Road, Bradford 1.
	Meetings: 3rd Mondays, 8 p.m.
	YORKSHIRE MAGICAL CLUB
	Trevor H. Hall, 8 North Park Road, Leeds 8.
	H.Q.: Conservative Club, Market Street, Bradford.
	Meetings: 1st Monday of month, 7.45 p.m.
Brighton:	REGENCY MAGICAL SOCIETY
	Sec.: G. E. Henty, 12 Reigate Road, Brighton 5.
	H.Q.: Regency Little Theatre, "Aylesbury," Furze Hill, Hove.
	Meetings: 2nd and last Wednesday in month, 7.45 p.m.
	SUSSEX MAGIC CIRCLE
	Sec.: Wyndham Howard, 22 Arundel Street, Brighton 7.
	H.Q.: 68 North Road, Brighton.
	Meetings: alternate Thursdays, 8 p.m.
Bristol:	BRISTOL SOCIETY OF MAGICIANS
	Sec.: C. N. Parker, 42 Parkstone Avenue, Horfield, Bristol.
	H.Q.: Royal Hotel, College Green, Bristol.
Burton-on-Trent:	CIRCLE OF MAGICIANS
	Sec.: T. H. Cotton, 11 Newton Road, Burton-on-Trent.
	H.Q.: Salem Sunday School, Station Street, Burton.
	Meetings: alternate Thursdays, 7 p.m.
Cardiff:	WESTERN MAGIC CIRCLE
	Sec.: James Douglas, 4 Plasturton Avenue, Cardiff.
	H.Q.: Oddfellows Hall, Charles Street, Cardiff.
	Meetings: 1st Thursday of month, 7 p.m.
Cheltenham:	COTSWOLD MAGICAL SOCIETY
	Sec.: Serl Taunt, Witcombe Hostel, Shurdinton Road, Brock-worth, Glos.
	H.Q.: Victory Club, Nelson House, Trafalgar Street, Cheltenham.
	Meetings: 1st and 3rd Sundays in month, 2.30 p.m.
Coventry:	COVENTRY MAGIC CIRCLE
	Sec.: J. F. Brandrick, 305 Tile Hill Lane, Coventry.
	H.Q.: Maudsley Hotel, Allesley Old Road, Coventry.
	Meetings: 1st and 3rd Tuesday of month.

Derby: DERBY SOCIETY OF MAGICIANS
Sec.: Fred Wiles, 81 Nightingale Road, Derby.
H.Q.: Co-operative Hall, Nightingale Road, Derby.

Dewsbury: MYSTIC SEVEN
Sec.: Harold Beaumont, 9 Plane Street, Stile Common, Huddersfield.
H.Q.: Scarboro Hotel, Dewsbury.
Meetings: alternate Tuesdays, 7.30 p.m.

Doncaster: DAVID DEVANT MYSTIC CIRCLE
Sec.: E. Wales, 25 King Edward Road, Balby, Doncaster.
H.Q.: Woolpack Hotel, Market Place, Doncaster.
Meetings: alternate Wednesday evenings.

Dublin: MYSTIC CIRCLE OF MAGICIANS
Sec.: Joseph O'Donnell, 8 Inverness Road, Fairview, Dublin.
H.Q.: Grosvenor Hotel, Westland Row, Dublin.
Meetings: 3rd Saturday in month, 8 p.m.
SOCIETY OF IRISH MAGICIANS
Sec.: Miss Nita Kelly, Jury's Hotel, College Green, Dublin.

Edinburgh: EDINBURGH MAGIC CIRCLE
Sec.: J. Henderson, 18 Abercorn Drive, Edinburgh.

Emsworth: ASTRAL MAGICAL SOCIETY
Sec.: H. G. Smith, 5 Gordon Road, Emsworth, Hants.

Enfield: MERLIN MAGICAL SOCIETY
Sec.: A. Thwaites, 8 Bexhill Road, London, N.11.
H.Q.: Duke of Abercorn, Sydney Road, Enfield, Middlesex.
Meetings: alternate Thursdays, 8 p.m.

Exeter: EXONIAN MAGICAL SOCIETY
President: W. E. Browning, "Montreux," Pinhoe, Exeter.

Glasgow: SCOTTISH CONJURERS' ASSOCIATION
Sec.: Duncan Johnstone, 90 Kilberry Street, Glasgow N.

Halifax: HALIFAX MAGIC CIRCLE
Sec.: H. H. Greenwood, South Grove, Halifax.
H.Q.: Plummet Line Hotel, Bull Green, Halifax.
Meetings: last Wednesday of month, 8 p.m.

Harrogate: HARROGATE SOCIETY OF MAGICIANS
Huddersfield: HUDDERSFIELD CIRCLE OF MAGICIANS
Sec.: R. Ward, 25 Newsome Road, Huddersfield.
H.Q.: St. John's School, Hillhouse Lane, Huddersfield.
Meetings: alternate Mondays, 7.30 p.m.

Hull: HULL MAGICIAN'S CIRCLE
Sec.: F. W. Collison, 40 Hutt Street, Spring Bank, Hull.
H.Q.: Lord Collingwood Hotel, Lowgate, Hull.
Meetings: fortnightly.

Ilford.   ILFORD MAGICAL SOCIETY
              Sec.: Douglas Keen, 13 Mayfair Avenue, Ilford, Essex.
              H.Q.: Golden Pheasant Restaurant, Cranbrook Road, Ilford.
              Meetings: alternate Wednesdays, 7.30 p.m.

International: INTERNATIONAL BROTHERHOOD OF MAGICIANS
              British Ring, No. 25
              Sec.: W. G. Stickland, The Wand, Dudsbury Crescent, Ferndown, Dorset.
              INTERNATIONAL BROTHERHOOD OF MAGICIANS
              Irish Ring, No. 85
              Sec.: Jack Kearns, 2 New Road, Inchicore, Dublin.

Isle of Man: MAGICIANS OF MANN
              Sec.: Sir Alexander Cannon, Laureston Mansion House, Douglas, I.O.M.
              H.Q.: Laureston Mansion House.
              Meetings: 2nd Tuesday each month, 7.30 p.m.

Leamington Spa: LEAMINGTON AND WARWICK MAGIC CIRCLE
              Sec.: M. R. Averns, 16 Jury Street, Warwick.
              Meetings: alternate Tuesdays.

Leeds: LEEDS MAGIC CIRCLE
              Sec.: R. Hartley, 11 Crag Road, Horsforth, Leeds.
              H.Q.: Civic Theatre Meeting Rooms and Folly Lane Rooms, Beeston Hill, Leeds.
              Meetings: 2nd and 3rd Thursdays of month respectively, 7.30 p.m.
              LEEDS MAGICAL SOCIETY
              Sec.: George Horner, 57 Newlay Lane, Bramley, Leeds.
              H.Q.: Civic Arts Guild, 43 Cookridge Street, Leeds.
              Meetings: 2nd and last Tuesday of month, 7.30 p.m.

Leicester: BRITISH GUILD OF MAGICIANS
              LEICESTER MAGIC CIRCLE
              Sec.: J. F. Moore, 14 Eileen Avenue, Leicester.
              H.Q.: Bell Hotel, Humberstone Gate, Leicester.
              Meetings: 1st and 3rd Mondays of month, 7.15 p.m.

Liverpool: LIVERPOOL MAGIC CIRCLE
              Sec.: A. J. Sutton, 56 Delamore Street, Liverpool.
              H.Q.: Linwood Hall, Rice Street, Liverpool 9.
              Meetings: 2nd Thursday of month, 7.45 p.m.
              MAHATMA CIRCLE OF MAGICIANS
              Sec.: T. W. MacMinn, 11 Coombe Road, Irby, Wirral, Cheshire.
              H.Q.: Ocean Club, Lord Street, Liverpool.
              Meetings: 2nd and 4th Thursdays in month, 7.30 p.m.
              SORCERERS' SOCIETY
              Sec.: Fred Lowe, 75 Thornton Road, Liverpool 16.

London :   INSTITUTE OF MAGICIANS
H.Q.: Central Club, 127 Clerkenwell Road, E.C.1.
Meetings: every Thursday, 7 p.m.
LONDON SOCIETY OF MAGICIANS
Sec.: Geoffrey Robinson, Bristol House, 14 Southampton Row, W.C.1.
H.Q.: Conway Hall, Red Lion Square, W.C.1.
Meetings: Fridays, 7 p.m.
MAGIC CIRCLE
Sec.: Peter Newcombe, c/o Hearts of Oak Building, Euston Road, N.W.1.
H.Q.: Hearts of Oak Building, Euston Road, N.W.1.
Meetings: Mondays, etc., 6 p.m.
SOCIETY OF MAGICAL ENTERTAINERS
Sec.: Alex Weston, 195 Devonshire Road, Forest Hill, S.E.23.
H.Q.: Davenport Hall, Davenport Road, Catford.
Meetings: alternate Fridays, 8 p.m.
UNIQUE MAGICIANS' CLUB
Details from Harry Stanley, 14 Frith Street, W.1.
VAMPIRE MAGIC CLUB
Details from Max Andrews, 10/12 Archer Street, W.1.
ZODIAC MAGICAL SOCIETY
Sec.: F. Firth.
H.Q.: St. George's Hall, Y.M.C.A., Bond Street, Ealing, W.5.
Meetings: every Monday.

Manchester :   ORDER OF THE MAGI
Sec.: Wm. Hughes, 16 Lynton Drive, Burnage, Manchester.
H.Q.: Milton Hall, Deansgate, Manchester.
Meetings: 2nd Tuesday and 3rd Monday of month.
TOP HAT MAGICAL SOCIETY
Sec.: "Terry," 27 Salisbury Road, Chorlton-cum-Hardy, Manchester 21.
H.Q.: 27 Salisbury Road, Manchester 21.
Meetings: Saturday, 7 p.m.

Middlesbrough :   MIDDLESBROUGH CIRCLE OF MAGICIANS
Sec.: M. A. Marshall, 3 Lanehouse Road, Thornaby-on-Tees.
H.Q.: Temperance Institute, Woodlands Road, Middlesbrough.
Meetings: alternate Thursdays, 7.30 p.m.

Newcastle :   NEWCASTLE UPON TYNE MAGIC CIRCLE
Sec.: T. Cato, 51 Alderwood Crescent, Walkerville, Newcastle upon Tyne 6.
H.Q.: County Hotel.
Meetings: 1st Saturday, 2.30 p.m.; 3rd Tuesday, 7 p.m.

Northampton: NORTHAMPTONSHIRE MAGICIANS' CLUB
Sec.: F. H. Jones, 31 Cottarville, Weston Favell, Northants.
H.Q.: White Hart, Bridge Street, Northampton.
Meetings: 1st and 3rd Tuesdays each month, 8 p.m.

Nottingham: GUILD OF MAGICIANS
Sec.: Ken Scholes, 268 Wollaton Road, Beeston, Notts.
H.Q.: Central Y.M.C.A., Shakespeare Street, Nottingham.
Meetings: alternate Wednesdays, 7.15 p.m., and Saturdays, 3 p.m.

Plymouth: PLYMOUTH MAGICIANS' CLUB
Sec.: Desmond Leach, 9 Hill Crest, Mannamead, Plymouth.

Portsmouth: INSTITUTE OF MAGICIANS
Sec.: Bob Marvo, 5 Unicorn Terrace, Landport, Portsmouth.
H.Q.: Nelson Tavern, Unicorn Road.
Meetings: every Friday.

Prestatyn: NORTH WALES MAGIC CIRCLE
Sec.: A. L. Williams, Langholme, Gronant, Prestatyn.
H.Q.: Toc H Hut, Fforddisa, Prestatyn.
Meetings: first Friday each month, 7 p.m.

Reading: HOME COUNTIES MAGICAL SOCIETY
Sec.: Reg. Wright, 84 Bulmershe Road, Reading.
H.Q.: George Hotel, Reading.
Meetings: 2nd Tuesday each month, 7.30 p.m.

Rochester: MEDWAY MAGICAL SOCIETY
Sec.: Phil Lines, 3 Mill Road, Gillingham, Kent.
H.Q.: King's Head Hotel, High Street, Rochester.
Meetings: alternate Tuesdays, 7 p.m.

Sheffield: SHEFFIELD CIRCLE OF MAGICIANS
Sec.: T. C. R. Harrison, 116 Gleadless Common, Sheffield.
H.Q.: Grand Hotel, Leopold Street, Sheffield 1.
Meetings: alternate Tuesdays, 7.30 p.m.

Slough: WIZARDS OF THE SILVER STAR
Sec.: Travis B. Wills, 9 Nursery Way, Wraysbury, Middlesex.
H.Q.: Royal Hotel, Station Approach, Slough.

Southampton: ASSOCIATED WIZARDS OF THE SOUTH
Sec.: S. Ivan Simpson, Sailors' Home, Oxford Street, Southampton.

Southport: SOUTHPORT MAGIC CIRCLE
Sec.: Eddie Dexter, 14 Derwent Avenue, Southport.
H.Q.: St. Andrew's Hall, Eastbank Street, Southport.
Meetings: 1st and 3rd Thursdays of month, 7.45 p.m.

Southsea: PORTSMOUTH AND DISTRICT MAGIC CIRCLE
H.Q.: Tynings Hotel, 3 Eastern Parade, Southsea, Hants.

Stoke-on-Trent: MERCIAN MYSTICS SOCIETY
Sec.: David Roxburgh, 35 Aynesley Road, Shelton, Stoke-on-Trent.
H.Q.: Blue Bell Hotel, Hanley.
Meetings: 2nd and 4th Mondays, 7.30 p.m.

Tenby: PEMBROKESHIRE SOCIETY OF MAGICIANS
Sec.: Roy Davies, 19 The Green, Tenby, South Wales.

Wakefield: THE MYSTIC TRIANGLE
Sec.: S. Lowles, 19 Haggs Hill Road, Ossett, Yorks.
H.Q.: Blue Circle Club, Silver Street, Wakefield.
Meetings: 1st and 3rd Mondays each month.

Watford: WATFORD ASSOCIATION OF MAGICIANS
Sec.: Eddie Long, 6 Hastings Way, Croxley Green, Herts.
H.Q.: Old Free School, George Street, Watford.
Meetings: alternate Mondays 8 p.m.

West Hartlepool: TEES-SIDE MAGICAL SOCIETY
Sec.: Clive Allen, 185 Hart Lane, West Hartlepool, Co. Durham.
H.Q.: York Road Methodist Hall.
Meetings: 2nd and 4th Thursdays, 8 p.m.

Wolverhampton: WOLVERHAMPTON CIRCLE OF MAGICIANS
Sec.: Donald G. Crombie, 4 Westland Avenue, Wolverhampton.
H.Q.: Friends' Meeting House, Horsman Street, Wolverhampton.
Meetings: alternate Wednesdays, 7.30 p.m.

Worcester: WORCESTER WIZARDS
Sec.: A. Cole, 45 Vauxhall Street, Worcester.
H.Q.: Barbourne Inn, New Bank Street, Worcester.

York: YORK SOCIETY OF MAGICIANS
Sec.: C. Allison, 20 Westfield Terrace, Tadcaster, Yorks.
H.Q.: Rechabite Hall, York.
Meetings: monthly, Thursdays, 7.30 p.m.

MANUFACTURERS AND SUPPLIERS OF MAGICAL APPARATUS*

Aberdeen Joke Factory, George Street, Aberdeen.
Abraxas Studio, 3 Central Drive, Barnton, Northwich, Cheshire.
Andrews, Max, 10/11 Archer Street, London, W.1.
Andrews, Val, 374 King's Road, London, S.W.3.
Baker, Roy, 45 Salisbury Avenue, Rainham, Kent.
Blake, George, 9 St. Albans Road, Leeds 9.
Bradford Magic Studio, 139 Leeds Road, Bradford 3.
Carlos Magic Studio, 58 North Road, Brighton.
Chavel Magic Corner, Ramillies Arcade, Oxford Street, London, W.1.
Clarke (Tony) Novelties Ltd., 182 South Lambeth Road, London, S.W.8.
Clive, Paul, Back 68 Cocker Street, Blackpool.
Davenport, L., and Co., 35 New Oxford Street, London, W.C.1.
de Hempsey, Sydney, 363 Sandycombe Road, Kew Gardens, Surrey.
de Seevah, Henri, 1 Clarence Road, Harborne, Birmingham 17.
Devano, 26 Sheridan Road, Bexleyheath, Kent.
Ellisdon Bros. Ltd., 245/7 High Holborn, London, W.C.1.
Gamage, A. W., Ltd., Holborn, London, E.C.1.
Goldston, W., 10 West Central Street, London, W.C.1.
Hamley Bros. Ltd., 200/202 Regent Street, London, W.1.
Hughes, Jack, 2 Evelyn Avenue, Colindale, London, N.W.9.
Kaymar Magic, 59 Hunts Mead, Billericay, Essex.
Kharduni's Magic Shop, 56a King Street, Wallasey, Cheshire.
Loyal Novelty Supplies, 41 Waverley Crescent, Gidea Park, Essex.
Mac's, 49 The Front, Seaton Carew, West Hartlepool.
Magical Exchange Service, 1a Ribble Road, Central Drive, Blackpool.
Magician's Mecca, 255 Broad Street, Birmingham.
Mephisto Magic, 2/4 Lennox Road, Walthamstow, London, E.17.
Merlin's Workshop, Back 28 Clapham Road, Lowestoft.
Oswald, Oscar, 5 Duke Street Hill, London, S.E.1.
Presto Magic, 110 Devonport Road, London, W.12.

* Reproduced from *The Magician's Diary and Year Book, 1956,* by kind permission of the publishers, The Penshaw Press, 59 Hunts Mead, Billericay, Essex.

Renaud, 1 Philip Street, Bath.
Scottish Magic Studio, 1 India Buildings, Victoria Street, Edinburgh 1.
Stanyon, Ellis, 76 Solent Road, West Hampstead, London, N.W.6.
Supreme Magic, 31 Clifton Street, Bideford, Devon.
Unique Studio (Harry Stanley), 14 Frith Street, London, W.1.
Wizardo Novelty and Book Co. (Edward Beal), 235 Lake Road, Portsmouth.

MAGICAL PUBLISHERS AND BOOKSELLERS

Arcas Magical Publications, 404/8 Sydenham Road, Croydon, Surrey.
Armstrong, George, 62 Wellington Road, Bush Hill Park, Enfield, Middlesex.
Findlay, J. B., Crescent Road, Shanklin, Isle of Wight.
Fleming Book Company of U.S.A.: Details from Robertson Keene, The College, Shalfleet, Isle of Wight.
Goodliffe, 15 Booth Street, Birmingham 21.
Jenness, George, 47 Inverness Avenue, Enfield, Middlesex.
Magic Book Club, 59 Hunts Mead, Billericay, Essex.
Penshaw Press, 59 Hunts Mead, Billericay, Essex.
Thomas, Stanley, 3 Cassiobury Park Avenue, Watford.

LIST OF MAGICAL PERIODICALS*

Abracadabra Weekly, Saturdays. Published by Goodliffe the Magician, 15 Booth Street, Birmingham 21.
9d. per copy, £2 4s. per annum.

The Gen Monthly. Published by Harry Stanley, Unique Magic Studio, 14 Frith Street, London, W.1.
2s. per copy, £1 per annum.

Hughes' News Quarterly. Published by Jack Hughes, 2 Evelyn Avenue, Colindale, London, N.W.9.
Subscription, one year, 2s. 6d.

Magic Magazine Monthly. Published by Max Andrews, 10-11 Archer Street, London, W.1.
1s. 6d. per copy, 15s. per annum.

The Magic Wand Quarterly. Published by George Armstrong, 62 Wellington Road, Bush Hill Park, Enfield, Middlesex.
7s. 6d. per copy, £1 10s. per annum.

Magical Digest Monthly. Published by Oscar Oswald, 5 Duke Street Hill, London, S.E.1.
1s. 6d. per copy, 15s. per annum.

Pentagram Monthly. Edited by Peter Warlock, published by George Armstrong, 62 Wellington Road, Bush Hill Park, Enfield, Middlesex.
1s. 6d. per issue. Subscription: 6 months 9s. 6d.; 12 months 18s.

The Wizard Published by George Armstrong, 62 Wellington Road, Bush Hill Park, Enfield, Middlesex.
2s. per copy. Subscription: 6 months, 12s. 6d.; 12 months, £1 4s.

World's Fair (Page of magicians' news) Weekly. All newsagents. 4d. per copy.

* Reproduced from *The Magician's Diary and Year Book, 1956*, by kind permission of the publishers, The Penshaw Press, 59 Hunts Mead, Billericay, Essex.